Just Enough Project Management

The Indispensable Four-Step Process for Managing Any Project Better, Faster, Cheaper

Curtis R. Cook, Ph.D., PMP

McGraw-Hill

New York   Chicago   San Francisco   Lisbon
London   Madrid   Mexico City   Milan   New Delhi
San Juan   Seoul   Singapore   Sydney   Toronto

The McGraw·Hill Companies

Copyright © 2005 by The McGraw-Hill Companies, Inc. All rights reserved. Printed in the United States of America. Except as permitted under the United States Copyright Act of 1976, no part of this publication may be reproduced or distributed in any form or by any means, or stored in a data base or retrieval system, without the prior written permission of the publisher.

5 6 7 8 9 10 DOC/DOC 0 9 8 7 6 5

ISBN 0-07-144540-4

Product or brand names used in this book may be trade names or trademarks. Where we believe that there may be proprietary claims to such trade names or trademarks, the name has been used with an initial capital or it has been capitalized in the style used by the name claimant. Regardless of the capitalization used, all such names have been used in an editorial manner without any intent to convey endorsement of or other affiliation with the name claimant. Neither the author nor the publisher intends to express any judgment as to the validity or legal status of any such proprietary claims.

PMBOK is a registered trademark of Project Management Institute, Inc.

McGraw-Hill books are available at special quantity discounts to use as premiums and sales promotions, or for use in corporate training programs. For more information, please write to the Director of Special Sales, Professional Publishing, McGraw-Hill, Two Penn Plaza, New York, NY 10121-2298. Or contact your local bookstore.

 This book is printed on recycled, acid-free paper containing a minimum of 50% recycled, de-inked fiber.

Dedication

This book is dedicated to my wife and best friend Cindy, who for 25 years has supported and believed in me when I said, "You know, I am going to write a book on project management ...."

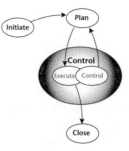

Contents

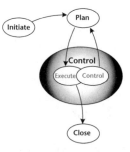

Foreword

I N *JUST ENOUGH PROJECT MANAGEMENT*, CURTIS COOK HAS
successfully translated a body of knowledge meant for
large, complex projects into a language that everyone
involved with projects can understand and apply to their
everyday project work. While remaining consistent with *A
Guide to the Project Management Body of Knowledge
(PMBOK Guide)*, the American National Standards
Institute standard for project management, the book
reduces its many processes to four easily understood and
practical steps.

Just Enough Project Management features templates
and checklists that can be put to immediate use. It is therefore a very useful guide to anyone who tackles short-term
activities with specific, measurable outcomes—in other
words, projects.

Beginning with an excellent introduction to projects
and project management, *Just Enough Project Management*
quickly gets down to business. Chapter 2 on initiating a
project provides a clear, concise Project Charter template,
complete with instructions on how to fill one out for the
reader's own project. From there, the book delves into the
both the essentials of project planning in Chapter 3 and

more advanced concepts of planning in Chapter 4. Chapter 4, especially, provides excellent guidance on how to create realistic schedules, how to overcome political pressures, how to anticipate risks, and how to account for statistical realities so as to produce a project plan that may actually be achievable (rare in our society).

Chapter 5 delves into the realities of controlling the project once the baseline plan has been approved. There the reader will find more on controlling changes, dealing with team challenges, managing the customer relationship, and keeping the project on track. Chapter 6 continues the practical theme of the book by providing a simple, easy-to-follow process for gaining customer acceptance of the deliverable, capturing lessons learned, celebrating team success, and transitioning the project to continuing operations and support.

In Chapter 7, the book shifts gears to a much-needed treatment of juggling multiple small projects. Cook provides an excellent, yet conceptually simple model for dealing with project overload and managing multiple projects.

The book concludes with an excellent glossary of key terms and an entertaining and highly informative annotated bibliography.

In *Just Enough Project Management* Curtis Cook has created a practical, easy-to-use guide for managing projects. It will serve as an excellent handbook or resource for anyone involved in managing projects, especially those with little formal training or experience. Simply stated, this book is a must read for anyone who manages projects and wants to bring his or her projects in on time, within budget, according to specifications—without all the red tape.

—David I. Cleland, Ph.D., PMP
Professor Emeritus
University of Pittsburgh

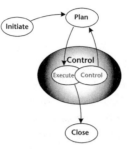

Introduction

MOST PEOPLE TODAY ARE INVOLVED IN PROJECT WORK IN some capacity, but for the majority of us, using formal project management techniques on our average-sized projects is like hiring an accounting firm to balance our checkbooks. Could they do it? Sure—but it would be overkill. And yet, when used in proper proportion, project management principles and techniques can be invaluable even on small projects—especially when you manage half a dozen of them! Welcome to *Just Enough Project Management*.

Over the past decade, project management has become more popular as an approach to managing those finite work efforts we call "projects." But unfortunately, the practice is often perceived as overly bureaucratic and cumbersome, adding little value. In the January 2004 issue of *PM Network*, "Nix the Spreadsheet" (page 19), Tom Peters stated,

> With the advent of information technology, project managers have become much too focused on compli-cated charts and graphs and not intent enough on the overall business value.... We shouldn't always be

bogged down in the details and lose sight of the bigger picture.

My own observations over the past 30 years support Peters' conclusions. I have seen project management grow from an ad hoc application of common sense to the overapplication of complex processes. Many organizations have embraced project management but have adopted the "700-page-book approach" with dozens of process steps and associated inputs, outputs, and tools and techniques. Yet the statistics cited by major research firms tell us that fewer than 50 percent of our projects achieve their objectives. Why?

The answer is pretty obvious. Just as Peters suggests, project managers have become "buried in the part," spending too much time chasing down data and packaging it to report to management, and not enough time actually solving problems and adding value. Keep in mind that the underlying value of project management is in how efficiently and effectively it transforms strategic objectives into business results. Yet ironically, the profession and practice have become associated with bureaucratic processes. I say "ironically" because the driving force behind the genesis of project management was the desire to cut across bureaucracies to get the job done!

What happened? In the early days of project management, project teams achieved great success. James Tobin's entertaining and informative book *Great Projects* (Free Press, 2001) is full of examples of teams achieving great things as diverse as harnessing the Mississippi River to creating the Internet. Because of the obvious success of this approach, the concept grew and began to be applied to all projects, not just large ones. The Project Management Institute (PMI) was born in the 1980s. The PMI Standards Committee wrote and published *A Guide to the Project Management Body of Knowledge (PMBOK Guide)*, which described 39 processes and subprocesses, and provided a swarm of tools and techniques. Certification programs were instituted, the premier credential being the Project Management Professional (PMP) designation. Academic programs, including master's and doctoral degrees with concentrations in project management, were created. The idea seemed to be that if a person could attain PMP status or an advanced degree in project management, he or she would be an effective, if not great, project manager. And to the extent that this knowledge and structure are applied to large programs and supported by the proper software tools, it's a valid conclusion. But most projects are not major, and complex processes do not help managers of average-sized projects.

A friend of mine likes to say, "To a 4-year-old with a hammer, all the world is a nail." Armed with the *PMBOK Guide*, 100,000-plus project managers set out to manage every project using the "bible." But small projects don't need all the information and tools and techniques contained in the *PMBOK Guide*, and they definitely don't need foot-thick process manuals to achieve their objectives. *Just Enough Project Management* distils all the information "out there" into a few fast and easy techniques for those who manage average-sized projects and juggle multiple, small projects. There is no doubt that the project management mindset is extremely valuable when applied to any project, but we need to apply just enough project management to get the job done without all the red tape.

Is *Just Enough Project Management* for You?

This book is a practical, how-to guide for managing projects. If you are responsible for managing small to medium-sized projects, especially several simultaneously, this book is for you. Think of it as a step-by-step guidebook for managing projects. Follow the steps laid out here and you will experience a much higher success rate on your projects. Throughout the book, each step is broken down into a series of simple activities you can perform to move your project from the early start-up or initiation phase, through planning and control, and finally to a successful conclusion.

While it is not my intent to denigrate the PMI or the PMP credential, or for that matter advanced degrees (I am a PMP and have a Ph.D. in a field closely related to project management), the simple truth is that you do not need these credentials to successfully manage the vast majority of projects. What you do need is "just enough" project management to get the job done. That is the primary focus of this work.

This book also provides a nice overview of project management for those who manage project managers, for executives who sponsor projects and are responsible for the project management process, for the many people managing less-than-major projects, and for team members. The language of the Just Enough approach is consistent with that contained in the *PMBOK Guide*, and the steps are consistent with PMI's five process groups. This may be important if your organization has an extensive training program under way for project and program managers based on the *PMBOK Guide*. You will find the definitions of terms in the glossary similar to, and in many cases identical to, the generally accepted definitions in the *PMBOK Guide*.

Templates and Checklists

Throughout the book, a number of useful templates and checklists are provided to help you think about and create the documents needed to manage projects. Instructions on how to complete the templates are also provided, along with practical guidelines for their use on real projects. These templates are either Microsoft Word or Microsoft Excel documents and are easy to create.

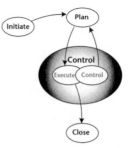

Acknowledgments

I WANT TO THANK MY EDITOR, LISA O'CONNOR, FOR HER enthusiastic support for this project. As the project manager for a book on project management, she continued to tell me that the material was interesting and useful to her, providing much-needed encouragement to this fledgling author.

Craig Sawin, chairman of the Novations Group, encouraged me to write the book from the first moment he saw a mock-up of the cover. I thank him and my many friends and colleagues at the Novations Group for their enthusiastic support.

Finally, I'd like to thank the team at J. Howard and Associates for being the first group to apply the principles of *Just Enough Project Management*. Naomi Sutherland and Kathy Lennox particularly were strong supporters of the simplified approach, and through their willingness to apply "just enough" project management to their own projects, I was encouraged to approach McGraw-Hill with the idea for the book.

1

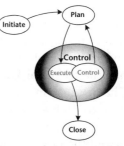

Project Management Overview

Thanksgiving at Beech Mountain

A COUPLE OF YEARS AGO OUR FAMILY DECIDED TO HAVE Thanksgiving dinner at our little 800-square-foot cabin in the beautiful high country of North Carolina. Beech Mountain, the town where we now live, is populated by 278 hardy souls, and in November it's crisp and cold—fireplace weather. The thought of having the whole family there with the smell of turkey cooking and sounds of the fire popping was really attractive. There was just one problem: The kitchen in our little cabin was just big enough for one person at a time—one of those spaces where, if the oven door was open, you couldn't open the refrigerator door. My wife agreed we should go, but she casually mentioned that we would have to eat out or bring in a turkey dinner since the kitchen was so small. As I recall, she said, "It's impossible to cook Thanksgiving dinner for 12 people in that kitchen." Naturally, because I'm a project manager, that's when I got interested. I volunteered to manage the "project" if she would be my subject matter expert (SME). She agreed. We had just launched our project!

1

To pull it off, I knew we would need a plan with all the activities coordinated, so I grabbed my laptop, fired up my project management software, took out all the recipe books, and with my wife (remember, she was the SME and actually had the technical knowledge) sat down to create the plan. The first task in project planning is to list all the tasks that have to be done to achieve success, so we created our task list (plan menu, shop, cook dinner, set table, etc.). Next, we put all the tasks in the order we would have to do them in to get the dinner prepared and served on time. Then we figured out who would do each task (we used our kids and parents as "resources"). Next we took a quick look at things that could possibly go wrong and added a few dollars and some time to the plan. Finally, we sat back, reviewed the plan, and decided we were ready to go. Planning finished! To make sure everyone would know what his or her part in the whole thing was, I printed out the task list and schedule (yes, including the critical path in red—I can't help it!). I taped it to the refrigerator in our cabin when we arrived and enjoyed the anticipation of watching people's reactions to finding out that they were on a project.

To make a long story short, everyone was actually pretty excited about being involved in our "project" and really got into it. The plan worked flawlessly with a little nudge here and there from me, the project manager. Once in a while we got behind, but we made up the time with a work-around here and there (project control). Dinner arrived on time, everyone felt proud of his or her contribution, and we enjoyed the perfect Thanksgiving Day. There was one lesson I learned the hard way, though: I forgot to add "cleanup" to the list of tasks, and as so often happens, the project manager got stuck with the dirty work! I added this to my mental "lessons-learned" file for future reference.

Just Enough Project Management

Did we apply too much or too little project management? Even though it sounds like we went overboard, in fact, given the project and the technical experience level of the project manager and team, we applied *just enough* to get the job done. Recall the steps:

1. **Initiate:** What is the challenge or problem?
2. **Plan:** How should we go about it?
3. **Control:** Are we on track?
4. **Close:** Finish the job, assess how we did, and capture lessons learned.

Figure 1-1 shows these four steps as part of a single overall process.

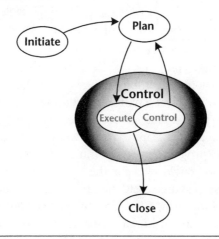

Figure 1-1. Four steps of project management

Notice that the control step includes executing the work and controlling any variances from the plan. The step is called *control* as opposed to *execute* because the role of the project manager while the work is being done is to monitor performance and identify variances from the plan, then take corrective action. Actual execution of the work itself is not a project management role, even if, as so often happens on small projects, the project manager is also doing some or most of the work. In the Just Enough approach, we focus on how the project manager controls the project, not on how to do the technical work.

Project Management as a Process

Project management is a process—a series of steps undertaken to achieve a specific outcome. All projects have a basic life cycle consisting of at least 4 steps. Depending on the industry and type of project, this basic model can be expanded (some pharmaceutical companies have 12-step processes), but it can't be compressed. The Just Enough approach is simply the application of these steps to any work effort we recognize as a project. It uses a few simple templates to guide our efforts to initiate, plan, control, and close a project. Here is a bit more detail on each step. (The remainder of the book will cover each one more fully.)

1. **Initiate the project.** The objective of this step is to recognize that a project should be done, determine what the project should accomplish, and formally launch the project with a Project Charter. It is during project initiation that the project manager is selected and given the authority to create the team that will work on the project.

2. **Plan the project.** Project planning is the process of developing a detailed plan for the project that includes the task list, resource assignments, schedule, budget, communication plan, risk plan, and change control process. This may sound like a lot of detail, but if you take a minute to think about it, you will realize that it is not too much detail. Even for projects around the house you have to know what steps to take to get the job done, how much money you have in your budget, who is going to do the work, and how much time the project will take. And you know that some things will go wrong, which will take up a little more time and money than you planned. It's the same for "official" projects at work—they just usually have more detail to reflect their larger size and complexity. Once the project sponsor approves the plan, it is known as the *project baseline*.

3. **Control the project during execution of the work.** Once the plan is approved, work begins. During this

step, the technical work is performed according to the plan, and any variances are identified and acted on to keep the project on track. The project manager coordinates and communicates with the project team and senior management and makes sure that the work is done on time, within budget, according to the project specifications and requirements. Project status reports are generated to keep stakeholders informed.

4. **Close the project.** This final step consists of three distinct activities:
   - **Hand off.** Ensure that the deliverable is handed off to the customer.
   - **Recycle.** Make sure that the hard-earned lessons learned during the project are passed on to others.
   - **Celebrate.** Reward the team and celebrate success.

The closing process includes a few last-minute checks to ensure that everything is in order and all project requirements have been satisfied.

A Few Basics before Proceeding

It is useful to think of a project as any undertaking with a *defined starting and ending point* and *specific, well-defined objectives* that, when attained, identify completion. In practice, for most projects there are limited resources and a limited amount of time in which to accomplish the objectives. This setup is so typical that it is even given a name—the *triple constraint*, as shown in Figure 1-2.

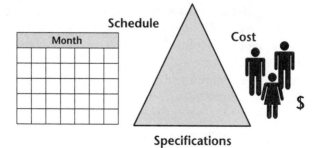

Figure 1-2. Triple constraint

Within the triangle is the *project scope*, which defines the boundaries of the project in terms of the technical requirements or specifications and the limits on time and cost. Interestingly, it is the constraints that make it a project! Without limits on money, resources, or time, there would be little need for project management. Of course in the real world there are always constraints, and there is always a need to find efficient ways to get work done faster, cheaper, and better. Keep in mind that the tighter the constraints, the greater the need for project management.

Once we realize that what we are working on is a project, we can use the discipline of project management to do the work. The Project Management Institute (PMI) defines project management as "The application of knowledge, skills, tools, and techniques to project activities to meet the project requirements."[1] Most successful project managers boil it down further.

> Project management is getting the job done on time, within budget, according to the specifications!

The Value of Project Management

Senior managers frequently ask me why anyone would want to adopt project management. After all, business as usual is more comfortable. And let's face it, most people don't like change, and they especially don't like operating within constraints—so why elect a management approach that deals with constraints and requires a rigorous approach to managing change? The simple answer is that the competitive environment most companies find themselves in requires a more disciplined approach to gaining market share or even surviving. And for nonbusiness projects, this approach simply helps us get organized. But there are other specific, documented reasons to use project management that we'll cover here before proceeding.

Reason 1. It establishes a single point of contact and accountability for the overall success of the project. Project management simply doesn't work unless the project manager is given authority to match his or her responsibility and accountability. One of the driving forces behind project management is the obvious advantage of empowering a project team to get a job done without having to worry about the usual managerial burdens associated with managing part of the organization. By putting one person in charge, project stakeholders—especially the customer—know who to go to with questions during design, development, production, test, and deployment. Let's look at authority, accountability, and responsibility a little more closely, since they are such important concepts.

Authority is the right to impose a degree of discipline. An army commander has the formal, legitimate authority to force compliance with his or her orders. The president of a company has this same authority. Unless people comply with the "orders" of a formal leader, there could be discipline or dismissal. Project managers have very little formal authority since they are typically leading teams of resources who do not report directly to them. However, project managers are able to borrow the necessary formal authority from the senior manager who sponsors the project through a formal document we will cover later called the *Project Charter*. Keep that document in mind as we continue.

Accountability means that the project manager is answerable for producing visible evidence of progress. In other words, the project manager is accountable for results, usually manifested in a physical product or the delivery of a service. When people say they are "accountable," they mean they are expected to "deliver the goods."

Responsibility is an obligation to act with or without guidance or formal authority. It's almost a moral obligation to do the right thing. That's why the management books say you can't delegate responsibility—it's an underlying obligation. A project manager who understands the project objective and is committed to achieving it feels responsible for the outcome—a sense of ownership for the project.

Putting these three concepts together—authority, accountability, and responsibility—it is easy to see why a project manager can be held accountable for producing results only if the proper authority is given to get the job done and he or she feels a sense of responsibility for the outcome. It turns out that leading project managers is a difficult task!

Reason 2. It focuses on meeting customer needs and expectations. If the project manager is given the appropriate authority, he or she is empowered to work closely with the customer to understand the requirement and to maintain a continuous dialog during performance to ensure customer satisfaction. A customer will feel the difference when you adopt a project management approach because your success as a project manager is measured by how well you achieve the triple constraint—giving the customer what you agreed to provide within the budget and time constraints that govern the project.

Reason 3. It improves performance in time, cost, and technical areas. When an individual's sole responsibility—upon which his or her future promotion depends—is to bring a project in on time, within budget, according to the specifications, he or she will either do it or "die trying," as the saying goes. Sometimes the best thing management can do once an experienced project manager has been put in charge of a project is to stay out of the way! This has a downside effect in that the pressure on team members can be intense—but it does clarify expectations and get results.

Reason 4. It obtains consistent results through the definition and application of a process across the business unit. As most people familiar with the quality movement can attest, application of a good, tight process to a problem helps eliminate waste and inefficiency. When that process includes best practices and is applied across a business unit, superior results will be achieved consistently. The problem in some organizations is that a process exists, but its use is voluntary. This makes little sense if the process can achieve better business results; yet in some organizations senior management spends money on process development but will not make its use mandatory. The only reason this might make sense is if the process is cumbersome and bureaucratic. In that case, the *Just Enough* approach will help!

Reason 5. It focuses on managing project scope and controlling change. We'll get into this in detail later, but a fundamental tenet of project management is that the project objectives and scope are defined early on and change is not permitted without requisite authority. This practically eliminates *scope creep*, which is defined as unconstrained scope change.

Reason 6. It helps avoid disasters by managing risk. Think of risk as anything that can derail the project—lack of resources, poorly defined requirements, customers who change their minds frequently, bad weather—you name it. In project planning, the team brainstorms all the possible negative impacts on the project and develops responses *before performance begins*. As a result, there are fewer surprises and disasters that threaten project completion.

Reason 7. It strengthens project teams and improves morale. Significant performance challenges create teams. One advantage of the constrained environment most projects operate within is that it creates an instantaneous performance challenge. As a result, project teams "gel" faster than functional teams. In addition, we human beings generally like to have a clear objective in our work. By definition, projects have specific, measurable goals and everyone knows his or her role in achieving the objective. Finally, we love closure. Projects have a defined beginning and an end. When the project is finished, we get to celebrate and enjoy that feeling of closure—of having finished something worthwhile. Taken together these three factors—challenging work, specific objective, and closure—lead to high morale on project teams.

Reason 8. It improves bottom-line performance and grows the business. This last reason is the result of the previous seven. Bottom-line results are improved because project teams are both more effective—they get the job done—and more efficient—they use fewer resources doing it. In addition, good project management results in higher customer satisfaction, leading to greater market share and revenue. Higher customer satisfaction, coupled with more efficient operations, leads to more profit.

Examples of Too Much Project Management

By now you are probably convinced you could use some project management. But what happens when we go overboard and apply too much project management for the size and complexity of the project? The answer is usually project failure, demoralized teams, and frustrated senior management. Let's take a look at a couple of real-world examples (names disguised, of course).

Our first example features a large company from the computer hardware industry. Company X was, at one point, one of the leaders in its field. Management decided, due to some pretty notable project failures, that they needed project management. Good decision. The first step they undertook was to assemble a team from around the world to develop a project management methodology. Another good idea. But as time passed, the scope of the methodology project expanded with little change control. The team added steps to handle almost every possible situation. Additional people, contractors, and especially money were poured into the project. The deliverable, when it finally arrived, was a huge process-oriented methodology document that filled three massive three-ring binders, a set of 22 pamphlets describing how to accomplish each of the hundreds of steps in the project, and a small booklet summarizing the whole process.

The headquarters team decided to make the process mandatory (again, nothing wrong with this if the methodology had been user-friendly). Literally everyone managing projects was sent a shrink-wrapped package containing all the literature with a notice that the process was mandatory. Admittedly, there was a matrix in the front of the first book that attempted to make the process scalable—use only certain parts for small, medium, and large projects—but the shock effect of seeing this massive shrink-wrapped set of books appear on your desk was a strong deterrent to even opening the package!

This company also spent millions of dollars training its project managers, but the training was generic, not tailored to the new methodology. Separate workshops were conducted to introduce people to the methodology, but after a handful of sessions, money for the effort dried up. After all, everything necessary for managing a project to completion was included somewhere in those books!

For the company's largest, most complex projects, the methodology and training paid off pretty well. A suitable software tool was used, and the people selected to run these major efforts knew how to do it and knew what parts of the methodology to use and what parts to ignore. But for the other 80 percent of the project managers assigned to small and medium-sized projects, the methodology was like an anchor. In an attempt to use the process and all the templates, project managers drowned in paperwork. Some projects simply stopped and teams drifted off—but the documentation was beautiful!

About a year after deployment of the methodology, the company did a global process audit to see what percentage of the project teams was using the methodology. The result? Less than 10 percent! Most project managers had resorted to homegrown approaches or regional and/or local processes that had existed before the advent of corporate guidance. As a result, some projects were successful and some were disasters, and essentially no improvement had taken place in the percentage of projects that were completed on time and within budget and that met the customer's requirements.

Within the next two years most of the people who had been involved with the initiative had been released or had moved on voluntarily to greener pastures. The company, now diminished, still had no company-wide process that provided just enough project management for small and medium-sized projects—the size of the majority of projects in a typical organization.

Our second example deals with a much smaller company—a dot-com in Southern California. As we all know, there were many reasons for the demise of some of these small Internet start-ups, but this one was killed in part by the application of too much process to average-sized projects. Company Y was started by a couple of entrepreneurs who at first had great success. Sales and profits grew, and so they were preparing for an initial public stock offering. During these preparations certain issues came to light. They realized that they couldn't afford to develop "toys," and let their customers play with them, and then decide whether to develop production systems on the most promising applications. Management felt a need for more consistency in their approach and more commercial successes. They needed to be able to predict their earnings better to impress the stock analysts who would evaluate their worth. So they brought in a consultant to help develop a project management process, set up a project office, and gain control of some of the projects that were overrunning their budgets and schedules. Not a bad idea....

The first sign of trouble came when an edict was decreed that all projects would be managed using a commercial software package. No training was provided on the tool, and no formal company-wide basic process for managing projects had been developed. The project office established a few guidelines, however. Every project required a multipage Project Charter, a detailed Project Plan that typically spanned over 15 pages, and complex reports, charts, and graphs, many of which were produced on a graphics package rather than project management software. Project managers spent all their time pushing paper. They soon became project administrators, not leaders, and they lost the respect of the people doing the work. Before long "project management" was seen as a non-value-adding bureaucratic process and was killed. The company returned to its ad hoc ways of managing its projects. It went out of business in 2002. Some of its competitors who had adopted Just Enough Project Management processes, forms, and procedures to plan and control their projects survived and are thriving to this day. I should know—they are my clients!

So project management adds value—but only when applied in the proper dosage. It is much wiser to apply a little, measure the success, then build up where needed into more sophisticated approaches than to drown your best and brightest in paperwork.

All Projects Need Project Management—But Just Enough to Get the Job Done!

OK—you are convinced that project management is good for you! Now it's time to dig into the Just Enough Project Management process and learn those fast, easy techniques for realizing all these benefits.

Note

1. Project Management Institute (PMI) Standards Committee, *A Guide to the Project Management Body of Knowledge*, (Upper Darby, Pa.: Project Management Institute, 2001), 205.

2

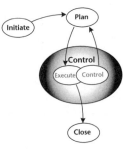

Initiating the Project

*P*ROJECT INITIATION IS THE PROCESS OF FORMALLY LAUNCH-
ing a project. The project manager verifies that all
the information needed to begin the project is on
hand, and he or she summarizes the information in the
Project Charter—the sole deliverable from this phase.
Think of each of the four steps in the project management
process as having inputs and outputs. The principal *input*
necessary to launch a project is a requirements document
of some sort. That can take one or more of several forms:

- Written specifications
- Customer contract
- Request for proposal
- Job order
- Service request
- E-mail directive
- Any other document expressing the need or objective of
  the project

The principal *output* is the approved Project Charter.

Figure 2-1 illustrates the activities the project manager
performs during the entire project management process,
with the initiation activities highlighted.

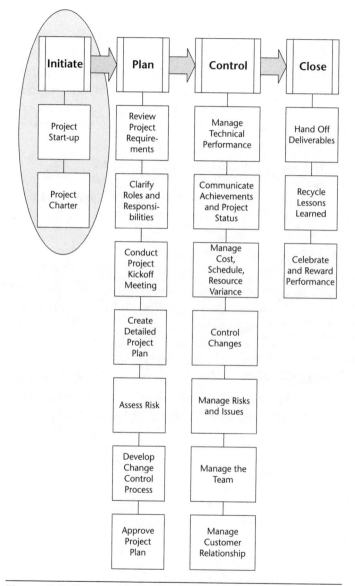

Figure 2-1. Process block diagram with the initiation steps highlighted

Is It a Project?

The first thing we need to decide is whether what you are working on is a project. Sounds simple, but I find a lot of confusion out there on this very important point. Recall the definition of a *project*—finite beginning and end, specific objective, and so on. Expanding this a bit produces a useful checklist you can use to determine whether the specific job you have in mind is a project:

- Does it have a clear beginning and end?
- Is there a specific, measurable objective?
- Is it a one-of-a-kind effort requiring a customized solution?
- Does it require a quick response?
- Does it require coordinating and managing several interdependent elements, organizations, or resources?

If the answer to these questions is yes, you have a project and project management will work for you. If not, you are performing ongoing work, governed by the normal policies and procedures within your organization.

Project Start-up

OK—it's a project. What next? Project start-up, which is relatively simple, yet very important. It focuses on determining who the key players are and understanding their roles and responsibilities. Ask yourself the following questions:

- Will I do all the work, or will others contribute?
- Who will be on the team?
- Who will use the end product?
- Who will specify the requirements?
- Who will approve the final product?
- Who's paying the bill?
- How available are the others involved?
- Do I have the authority to ask for help?

One simple way to get started is to draw a circle with you as the project manager in the middle and other participants in circles connected to you, as shown in Figure 2-2. At a minimum, identify these players:

- Project sponsor
- Project manager
- Key project stakeholders

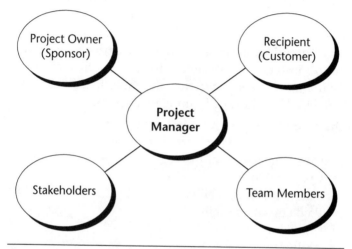

Figure 2-2. Project participants

Project Sponsor

The project sponsor is normally the person who can deploy and reprioritize resources and/or who provides funding for the project. The sponsor exercises final approval authority over project matters and ensures that any coordination and communication among senior managers takes place. By the time the project manager gets involved, the sponsor should be identified and should have, in fact, appointed the project manager. Sometimes this doesn't happen, and it is up to the project manager to find the "champion" for the project. Unless the sponsor is identified and is a champion, the project will fail—it's only a matter of time. *For this reason project managers should dig in their heels and refuse to go ahead with the project until the sponsor is identified.* This may sound strange, but remember, assertiveness is a positive trait in the project manager and is associated with success. Don't be afraid to do the right thing!

Project Manager

The project sponsor identifies a project manager with the relevant experience, competence, knowledge, and skill to successfully manage the project. What makes a great project manager? Various organizations have tried to nail down the competencies associated with success in the project environment. Most agree that the traits listed below are found in the highest-performing individuals:

Characteristics of Great Project Managers
- Commitment to the project and team
- Communication skill
- Customer focus
- Decision-making ability
- Problem-solving ability
- Conflict management ability
- Ability to energize others
- Ability to persuade and influence
- Ability to take the initiative
- Flexibility
- Leadership ability—that is, the ability to motivate others to *want* to do what the manager thinks is the right thing to do. Leadership ability includes such personal qualities as empathy, integrity, and honesty.

In addition to most of these characteristics, project managers must have sufficient authority to carry out their projects. They typically exercise broad responsibility and authority over their projects and perform the functions shown in Table 2-1.

Project Stakeholders

Once appointed, one of the first things the project manager does is identify all the project stakeholders—anyone who

Responsibility

- Act as the central point of contact for all formal, project-related communication
- Ensure that all project team members are aware of their responsibilities and commitments, and that they perform as promised
- Ensure that all contractual commitments are fulfilled on time, within budget, and to the customer's complete satisfaction and delight
- Prepare a realistic, detailed Project Plan and obtain agreement to the plan
- Maintain a Project Repository containing all relevant project information
- Control cost, schedule, and technical variance from the plan
- Report project status to management on a regular basis

Authority

- Authority to lead the project team
- Direct access to stakeholders on all matters pertaining to the project
- Authority to require periodic status reporting
- Authority to monitor the time, cost, and performance activities on the project and ensure that all problems are identified, reported, and solved
- Authority to cross functional organization lines and to interface with all levels of management as necessary to achieve project success
- Authority to renegotiate with functional managers for changes in resources

Table 2-1. Project manager's responsibility and authority

will be affected by the project. Every stakeholder will have a set of expectations, and it is the project manager's job to find out what they are and whether the project scope is sufficient to satisfy all stakeholders. If not, the project manager must manage expectations "up front" to avoid disaster later.

When in doubt as to whether an individual or organization in any area is involved in the project, the best course of action is to communicate directly with the individual in question. It's a good idea to develop a checklist for yourself of all potential stakeholders on a broad array of projects and use it every time you are on a project to make sure you don't miss anyone.

Establish the Project Repository or Binder

No one likes paperwork—but it is an unavoidable part of managing a project. Even on small projects the project manager should ensure that a *Project Repository* (which could be simply a binder) has been established and that all the important documentation generated in every step of the project has been filed in it. It can be as simple as a manila folder or as complex as an online document management system.

A checklist of some of the things that might be included in the Project Repository is provided in Table 2-2.

Before Proceeding, What Do You Need to Know?

Once all the key players have been identified and the project file has been set up, the project begins in earnest. The project manager should *always* ask the following five questions as he or she begins the project:

1. **What is it?** What are we going to produce? What is the deliverable?
2. **Who needs it?** Who is the customer?
3. **Why are we doing it?** What is the underlying problem we are trying to solve or opportunity we are pursuing?

- Project Charter
- Kickoff Meeting Documentation
- Project Plan
  - Work Breakdown Structure
  - Project Schedule
  - Project Budget
  - Resource Plan
  - Communication Plan
  - Change Control Plan
  - Risk Plan
- Status Reports
- Change Requests/Approvals
- Meeting Minutes
- Lessons Learned
- Closeout Checklist

Table 2-2. Project Repository contents

4. **Am I accountable for the project's success?** If I'm not, who is?
5. **What is my authority for making this happen?** If I don't have the authority, who does? Why don't I? How can I remedy this deficiency?

Unless the answers to these questions are known, the project should not proceed. Let me share an example of a project that almost failed due largely to the project manager's simply lacking the authority to get the job done.

The project was to renovate a landing strip that had deteriorated due to age, weather, and heavy use. A new generation of heavier airplanes was going to be using the runway, so it had to be repaved to handle the traffic. I was the project manager—or so I thought. Most of the work was going to be done by a contractor, so one of the first things we did was to issue a request for proposals and select a paving contractor. A Project Charter was never issued, and I didn't question my authority—I thought everyone knew I was "in charge." I was also much younger and more naïve than I am now!

I did notice that when I called a project status meeting, some of the key players from our engineering division would not attend, and I had a hard time getting the attention of the contractor's project manager. But I did the best I could and persevered. Everything was fine until the contractor got behind schedule. He began to pour concrete in the middle of the day when the temperature exceeded 100ºF (the project was in Phoenix, Arizona). This was not only bad trade practice but was in direct violation of the contract specifications. Water evaporated so quickly that cracks formed in the concrete and weakened it.

When I found out what was happening, I put on my hard hat and headed out to the job site with the senior engineer. Once we arrived, I told the contractor he would have to tear out the work that had been done and repour the concrete in the evening when the weather was cooler, as he had been doing. I noticed an exchange of furtive looks between our senior engineer and the contractor's project manager and began to "smell a rat." We adjourned our meeting without any commitments being made, and I confronted the senior engineer once we were back in the office. It turns out our engineer had approved the pour during the day as long as measures were taken to keep the moisture content of the concrete high enough to prevent cracking. Our engineer had approved a change to the contract without bothering to consult me or other team members to assess the impact on the project cost, schedule, or technical specifications. When I went to the "boss" to clarify my authority, I found out that the senior engineer really was "in charge" of the technical part of the job. The only problem was that neither I nor the rest of the team knew it!

Naturally I was upset, but more importantly the project almost failed. The contract had a damages clause in it for failure to meet the scheduled completion date and the technical specifications, but the engineer's actions partially relieved the contractor from their responsibility. Ultimately, the concrete did crack, and we were involved in a long legal battle to force the contractor to come back, tear up the runway, and do the job as specified in the contract. Had the change been processed correctly, we would never have approved the nonstandard process used, the runway would have been completed properly, and we would have saved the bundle of money we spent on legal fees.

The lesson here is that the project manager is responsible for the overall success of the project and must have the authority to lead the team and, when something like this happens, to take action to keep the project on schedule and in compliance with the technical specifications. In retrospect, the lesson I learned—which I've never forgotten—was to make sure I had the authority to manage a project before ever beginning it and to make sure all the team members knew their roles, responsibilities, and relative authority.

Project initiation, including completion of the charter, is the important first step toward gaining this understanding and launching the project in the right way.

The Project Charter

The best way to launch a project in such a way that both the sponsor and project manager know the purpose of the project and its linkage to strategy, other projects, and operations is to create a *Project Charter*. The charter *formally* recognizes the existence of a project, identifies the project sponsor, project manager, and other stakeholders, states the project objective and overall scope of the project, and includes many supporting details necessary for the sponsor to make a decision on whether to authorize the project. While the project sponsor is "officially" the originator of the charter, the project manager is usually tasked with preparing it for the sponsor's signature.

The main elements of a charter are shown in Figure 2-3 and are discussed below in sufficient detail to enable you to complete a charter immediately for your "real" projects. Even if you have projects under way without charters, it's a good idea to work through the charter elements to determine if you're missing any information. Doing this may enable you to explain why you're having problems on certain projects!

Project Charter	
Project Name	
Project Sponsor	
Project Manager	**Customer**
Other Project Stakeholders	
Stakeholder(s) Responsibilities	
Business Objectives	
Project Objectives (SMART)	
Deliverables	
Project Completion Date	**Budget**
Assumptions	
Link to Strategic Objectives and/or Other Projects	
We agree that this is a viable project. We authorize the beginning of the planning process.	
Project Sponsor	**Project Manager**

Figure 2-3. Project Charter

Project Name

This is self-explanatory, but if the project hasn't been named when you become involved, have some fun with it. When you get the team together for the first time, come up with a name that has some "zing" to it. Consider developing a motto or slogan that expresses the project objective. I've seen names and slogans like "The Liquidators—We Serve Beverages to Liquidate Your Thirst." Here's a cute motto I saw on a T-shirt for an underwater dive team: "Dive Deep, Live Shallow." You get the picture—have some fun!

Speaking of T-shirts, that's a great way to build team identity. Consider this story that demonstrates the "power of the T-shirt."

Andy Roddick, the American tennis phenomenon, had just completed a successful Wimbledon match in the 2004 tournament at the All-England Tennis Club. He was being interviewed on TV by a commentator and was wearing a Davis Cup T-shirt. Prior to this time Roddick had been noncommittal as to whether he would play on the Davis Cup team or participate in the Olympics, yet here he was on TV wearing the T-shirt. When asked whether he was looking forward to playing for the United States, he responded by saying something close to the following, "Yeah, it's just a lousy T-shirt, but when I got it, I realized that I was part of the team that would represent our country. It really charged me up, and I'm looking forward to being on the Davis Cup team."

The moral of the story? Things like T-shirts, coffee mugs, and other articles that help establish a team's identity are valuable ways to make a team tangible—to help the members realize that they are, in fact, a team and not just a group of talented individuals. Case in point: A millionaire tennis player with an attitude now feels as though he's part of the team. If it worked for the Davis Cup captain to enlist Andy Roddick, chances are it will work for you too!

Project Sponsor

Enter the name of the individual who is authorizing the project. The sponsor provides funds, prioritizes projects, and is at a level high enough to resolve resource issues.

Project Manager

Enter your name here! You are the person responsible for the overall success of the project.

Customer

Whether this is an internal or external project, it has a customer. This is the person or entity that is the principal beneficiary of your efforts. Enter the individual or the entity's name here.

Other Project Stakeholders

This is a crucial entry and one that is often overlooked. A stakeholder is defined as an individual or organization that is involved in or who will be affected by the project. Can you imagine not speaking to a key stakeholder during the start-up and planning of a project? It makes no sense, yet it happens all the time. If the project depends on stakeholders' providing resources on a project and they have not been consulted about this, they will naturally be upset and reluctant to cooperate. It is the sponsor's responsibility to coordinate with stakeholders before the project manager is even appointed. However, this sometimes doesn't happen. In these cases, it is up to the project manager to do the legwork. Identify all key stakeholders, go talk to them, and get their buy-in before the project gets under way. It's a wise investment of your time.

Stakeholder Responsibilities

List each stakeholder you talk to and his or her associated responsibilities on the project. Keep it brief—for example, you might enter, "George Johnson, Manager, Purchasing Division; execute contract for three analysts to support system design." Just a simple statement about the contribution of the stakeholders is enough for now to get the conversation with these key individuals going. They will let you know if you missed anything!

Business Objectives

What is the driving force behind this project? What is the business need? Write it down in this block. If you don't understand the linkage between this project and the business objective, find out before continuing.

Project Objectives

Every project, by definition, has an objective. But to be of any value in guiding the team and subsequently in evaluating the success of the project, a project objective has to be *SMART:*

Specific What exactly is the project about? What is the deliverable? What does the customer expect to see at the end of the project?

Measurable In the current era of project governance, more emphasis is being placed on defining, during the business case preparation, the metrics that will be used after the project to determine whether it's a success or failure. Are there performance parameters the deliverable must meet, functions that the item or system must perform, even levels of customer or user satisfaction that must be met? All these things are measurable.

Agreed All the key stakeholders must agree with the items on the Project Charter that either have an impact on them or that they will impact by providing resources or other help. The best way to ensure understanding is to communicate with them—just meet with each stakeholder and discuss the charter elements. Get their initials, signature, or e-mail confirmation that they agree with the project objectives.

Realistic Keep the objective reasonable and realistic, given the time and resources available—no "pie in the sky." When in doubt, talk to the sponsor. Most project managers are positive, can-do people, but this is the time for sober realism. Remember, you are setting expectations that you and the team will have to live with for the rest of the project.

Time Constrained Every project has a finite beginning and end. If not stated elsewhere in the charter, add the dates or performance period in this block.

Deliverables

List the specific deliverables that will be produced by the project team, including the following:

- A description of the hardware or tangible products to be used or created in the solution
- A description of the software to be used or created
- Identification of any services to be provided as part of the solution such as training, mentoring, on-site assistance, or follow-on warranty

When known, exclusions should be identified because stakeholders will usually assume that anything not explicitly excluded is included.

Project Completion Date

Add the completion date if known. If a date hasn't been set, something is wrong! Believe me, someone has a very clear expectation of when the project should finish, and it's your job as the project manager to dig it out and document it in the charter. Also identify, if possible, the major milestones that will be used to measure progress. If you don't know what they are at this point, don't worry about it. You'll meet with the team soon and hammer out the tasks and schedule.

Project Budget

Add the completion project budget, if known. Do *not* accept a "to be determined" statement. As in the completion date, someone—and it should be the sponsor—controls a finite budget for this project, and it must be stated in the charter. However, it could well be that the project is to be funded from a departmental budget and is not a separate project budget. Even in these cases, it's imperative that the project manager know how much money and other resources he or she can spend.

Assumptions

I can't overemphasize the importance of documenting the major assumptions underlying the other charter elements. List factors or situations you assume will or will not exist as you head into the planning phase. For example, if the availability date of a key resource is uncertain, the team should make a reasonable assumption about the date of availability and list this as an assumption. If you assume that all key resources will be available when needed, that funds will be provided, that scope changes will not occur—well, let's just say you should document everything here. Be careful not to assume away all the risks on the project. Your credibility will be challenged, and your dialog with the sponsor will be … interesting. Make reasonable assumptions, document them here, and discuss them with the sponsor. Your objective is to get a clear picture of the environment and challenges you will face in managing the project.

Linkage to Strategic Objectives and Other Projects

As shown in Figure 2-4, every project should be linked to a strategic objective of at least the business unit for which the project is being undertaken. And it should go without saying that every project is linked to at least one project, and quite likely several others. Unless the project manager and sponsor realize this, trouble will occur downstream when resource conflicts that cross project lines are felt. It is hard work to discover this information, but the investment pays off later in reduced chaos and smooth implementation.

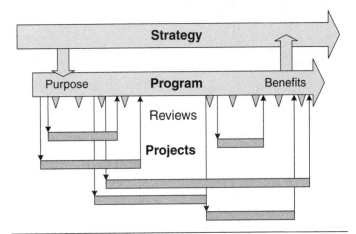

Figure 2-4. Strategic links to other projects

Sponsor Responsibilities and Signature

Once all the charter elements have been discussed and agreed to by the sponsor and key stakeholders, it is time for the sponsor to sign the document. Note that other stakeholders usually initial a coordination sheet or send an e-mail saying they have reviewed the charter and agree to support it. By signing the charter, the project sponsor signifies that he or she will provide the necessary funds to support the project and will perform the other responsibilities typically required of a sponsor, such as the following:

- Establishes and communicates the business case and alignment with the project
- Sets the scope and outlines clear expectations
- Selects and appoints a project manager
- Acts as a team mentor and is available and accessible
- Secures and supports the necessary budget
- Establishes the initial estimate of the project completion date
- Participates with the project manager in developing the project definition and charter
- Signs the Project Charter
- Participates in project reviews and problem solving

Distribution of the Charter

Once approved, a copy of the Project Charter should be distributed to project team members and internal stakeholders. It is not advisable to distribute the charter to external stakeholders, such as suppliers and consultants, if budgetary and risk information is confidential.

Transition to the Planning Phase

After the charter has been signed and distributed, the project manager is ready to begin building the project team, which will then help develop the Project Plan. If you are on a very small project, you and the team may be the same thing! Much of the information contained in the charter will carry over into the plan, but the plan is more detailed and provides the roadmap the team will use to complete the project successfully.

3

Project Planning Basics

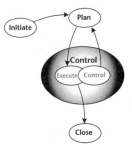

THE GUIDING PRINCIPLE OF PROJECT PLANNING IS TO KEEP it as simple as possible, given the size of the project. For small projects, the plan may consist of two or three pages, while on larger projects the plan will be much more comprehensive. The Project Plan is the roadmap for the entire project, and, regardless of the size of the project, it should include coverage of the following elements:

- **Project summary:** A short executive-level summary of the project origin and objectives
- **Work breakdown structure (WBS):** The task list
- **Resource assignments:** Who is going to do the work
- **Project schedule:** The detailed schedule and project completion date
- **Project budget:** How much money is allocated to the project
- **Risk assessment:** What could go wrong and what actions and reserves should be included in the plan to mitigate the highest-risk events
- **Communications:** How the team plans to communicate, meet, and report status
- **Change control process:** How changes will be handled

The best and quickest way to develop the plan is to assemble the project team and lead a brainstorming session to capture and record the information you need. Use simple techniques and materials, such as sticky notes or flipcharts, and then create a draft plan for review by the team. Once the team concurs with the draft, the project manager meets with the sponsor, makes any needed adjustments, and puts the plan in final form for the sponsor's approval. Once approved, the plan becomes known as the *baseline*. In this chapter we'll concentrate on the basics of project planning. In Chapter 4 we'll introduce more advanced techniques, such as critical path analysis, for use on more complex projects.

The Planning Process

The Project Charter is the principal input to project planning. It provides all the information the project manager needs to get going. Imagine for a moment what it would be like starting a project without this information—like shooting in the dark and hoping to hit the target. If you find yourself in this situation, it may be time to exercise one of the principal competencies of successful project managers—assertiveness! Make sure you have a signed charter.

Project planning is relatively straightforward. The project team decomposes the project objectives into a list of manageable "chunks" of work called a *work breakdown structure* (WBS) or, more commonly, a *task list*.

After the team creates the WBS, task dependencies are identified. On small projects this is somewhat intuitive and obvious, but on larger projects it's hard work. This action, along with calculating the duration of each task, will result in creation of the project schedule and will reveal the critical path. (We'll define and work with the critical path later.) Once resources have been assigned to tasks in the WBS, the project schedule can be refined, analyzed for risks, and prepared for approval.

Depending on the size of the project, the project team may produce a variety of subordinate plans, such as a risk plan, a communication plan, and a scope change control plan. On smaller projects these are simply sections or paragraphs in the overall Project Plan. Once all the information has been gathered and documented, the sponsor approves the plan and the team is authorized to move forward and execute the plan.

The major deliverable from the planning step is the Project Plan, which defines in detail:

- *What* is to be done (the WBS)
- *Who* will do the work (resource assignments)
- *When* the work will be accomplished (the project schedule)
- *How much* the project will cost (the budget)
- *How* the project will be managed in terms of scope change control, status reporting, and overall control of variances

Taken together with the Project Charter, the Project Plan pulls together in one place virtually everything that is known about the project.

How Much Time Should Be Devoted to Planning?

I am often asked how much time should be spent in planning. In our Western society we're usually in a hurry to get going. As a result, we spend little time planning and a lot of time fire fighting over the life of a project. In contrast, in Eastern cultures much more time is spent in planning and getting consensus before the work, but implementation is fairly smooth. Our goal is to devote just enough time to planning to get a clear understanding of what is required to achieve the project objective.

As a general rule of thumb, project teams should spend a minimum of 5 percent of the project duration on planning. It usually takes more than this, but that's a minimum. For example, let's say you want to build a new deck, and you think it will take you about 3 days (24 work hours) to actually build. Five percent of 24 hours is only 72 minutes. I spent more time than that planning Thanksgiv-ing dinner! Yet when we apply the rule of thumb to our work projects, we often get a strong negative reaction from management and team members on the amount of time we're spending on planning. We hear things like, "Let's just get going—there's no time to waste on fancy plans." What that really says is that we don't have time to plan, but we do have time to react to the negative consequences that will undoubtedly hit us if we don't do a good job planning the project up front. This is a good time to practice your assertiveness once again. Insist on taking a reasonable amount of time to plan the project, and you will save your-self a lot of time reacting to emergencies later.

Forming the Core Team

The most important element of a project is the team. The project team will plan, implement, and monitor the work being performed. The project manager is responsible for forming and maintaining a cohesive, functioning, moti-vated team capable of doing the work as planned.

Most new project managers who have been promoted from the technical ranks take people skills for granted, and, as a result, they fail to develop a high-performing team. While it is not within the scope of this book to go into great detail on team building, we can provide "just enough" information to get you started. For more information I highly recommend Dr. Jim Lewis's book, *Project Leader-ship* (see the Further Reading section).

At a minimum, however, you must accomplish the fol-lowing to have any chance of forming a cohesive team:

- Identify key team members based on the nature of the work.
- Obtain team members' commitment. (If it's too early in the project for the actual team members to be known, obtain a commitment from the resource providers. If

you have done a good job of coordinating the Project Charter with stakeholders, this should not be difficult.)

- Assign roles and responsibilities within the team.
- Ensure that the team has the necessary resources.
- Conduct a kickoff meeting to make the team tangible and generate excitement and commitment (and pass out those T-shirts!).

The project manager must be directly involved with the team's day-to-day interaction and operation. Leadership is perhaps the most significant skill that the project manager brings to the project, and the use of that skill must *always* be evident. As the project manager, you—not the functional manager—are responsible for motivating, encouraging, and leading the team. While the project is underway, you're the de facto boss. Building an effective team is a prerequisite for the project to go forward; without it, the project cannot succeed.

Planning Activities

Figure 3-1 illustrates the activities the project manager performs during the second step, project planning. We'll take each one in turn so that by the end of this chapter you will be able to write a Project Plan for your real projects.

Review Project Requirements

An old project management axiom says, "Don't solve the wrong problem in a perfect way." This simply means that you should take the time to think through the plan before jumping into project execution. And the first step in the planning process is to take a fresh look at the project requirements, talk to the customer, and verify that nothing has changed since the Project Charter was put together. That's it: Just verify that you are solving the right problem!

Clarify Roles and Responsibilities

We've already spent quite a bit of time figuring out who is on the team, but this is the point at which the project

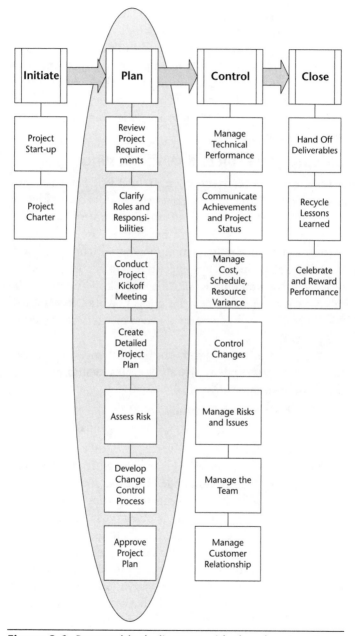

Figure 3-1. Process block diagram with the planning steps highlighted

manager takes a deep breath, looks at the overall project objectives and constraints, and decides whom he or she wants on the team. It's always a combination of whom you want and who is available, and strictly speaking, it is up to the functional managers to assign the right people to your project. But this is your chance to choose your team and begin to work with them to understand the various roles and responsibilities.

Conduct the Project Kickoff Meeting

After the project team members are identified and assigned to the project, the next step is to conduct the "kickoff meeting." This meeting is an introduction to the project for team members who were not part of the preliminary planning effort, for management personnel who are providing the team members, for executive management, and for other project stakeholders. At the kickoff meeting, the project manager describes the project, works to establish team identity, and generates a sense of excitement about the project.

As the project manager, the kickoff meeting is your first opportunity to demonstrate your leadership, so follow these three simple rules:

1. Start the meeting on time.
2. Achieve the objectives by using an agenda.
3. Finish the meeting on time.

Simple, isn't it? But when is the last time you attended a meeting that started and ended on time and achieved its objectives? Be honest! In project management, things start and end on time and meet their objectives. At the kickoff meeting you are demonstrating these values, so get it right!

The format for the kickoff meeting is driven by project size and complexity—the larger the project, the more formal the meeting. For most projects, a simple agenda and maximum of 1 hour's time are all that's necessary to get the project off to a good start. And for virtual teams on small projects, a phone call might do the trick.

At the kickoff meeting, the project manager should establish an atmosphere of challenge, teamwork, and collaboration among team members. Team members should be excited about the project and their individual roles. Consider using the checklist in Table 3-1 to make sure everything is covered as you prepare for the meeting.

❏ Prepare a summary of the meeting's goals, highlighting opportunities this project will present to organization and to team members. Cover any special aspects of the project that might present challenges beyond the ordinary.

❏ Prepare an overview of the project that summarizes the business requirements and the current plans for meeting those requirements. Ensure that the overview addresses the Project Charter elements, including any time or budget constraints. Bring the team up to date on project accomplishments.

❏ Arrange for the project sponsor to speak for 10 to 15 minutes on his or her perspective on the importance of the project.

❏ Discuss roles and responsibilities of all team members and other stakeholders, if any.

❏ Discuss communication. What information needs to be exchanged? Who needs to have it? What form will it take? When will project meetings take place?

❏ Using the project schedule from the charter as a guide, discuss schedule challenges and how the team can meet the scheduled completion date. Present the project deliverables, and discuss key milestones.

❏ Schedule a planning workshop for the core team to create the Project Plan.

❏ Determine what follow-on action is required from the kickoff, and plan to assign responsibilities accordingly so that project planning may proceed.

❏ Bring food!

Table 3-1. Kickoff meeting checklist

I mentioned an agenda earlier. To ensure that all items are covered during this meeting—it may be one of the few times all key individuals in the project will be together in one location—use an agenda and stick to it during the meeting. Figure 3-2 shows an agenda I have used for the past two decades. It works, so please feel free to use it for your actual projects.

It's good practice to make a few notes during the meeting and distribute these, along with any action items, to attendees after the meeting. In many cases the project manager will conduct a detailed project planning meeting immediately after the kickoff. Remember to notify key project team members in advance, since planning sessions take more time than a simple kickoff meeting.

Note: Make sure the project sponsor has an opportunity to participate in the kickoff meeting. This is an opportunity for the sponsor to demonstrate support for the project and team and to explain how the project fits into the larger mission and strategy of the organization.

Create the Work Breakdown Structure (WBS)

The term *work breakdown structure* is an imposing but widely used phrase that simply means a list of tasks that must be performed. A WBS is a family tree of all the project work required to deliver an end product or service. It provides the structure for planning and controlling the entire project throughout its life cycle.

The WBS is the key to the rest of the planning process and is used for scheduling, budgeting, resource assignments, scope change control, variance analysis and control, and status reporting. Most organizations accomplish the same general types of projects repeatedly. As a result, teams will very seldom have to create a WBS from scratch. It's a good idea to keep copies of the most common work breakdown structures you have created on hand for future use. If your organization has a project office or other organization that maintains lessons learned and provides internal help to project managers, samples of WBSs should be available there.

DOCUMENT PREPARATION INFORMATION

Project Name	Project Manager	Date Prepared

SPONSOR INFORMATION

Sponsor	Contact Information

ATTENDEES

Name	E-mail or Other Address

MEETING INFORMATION

Date	Start Time	End Time	Location

Meeting Purpose

AGENDA ITEMS	PRESENTER	TIME
Welcome and Introductions		
Executive Perspective		

Project Overview
   Project Objectives
   Project Charter Elements
   Proposed Solution
   Project Deliverables
   Project Accomplishments
    to Date		

Project Schedule and Major Milestones		
Team Roles and Responsibilities		
Communication Plan		
Special Issues		
Summary and Close		

Figure 3-2. Kickoff agenda template

Notice the first few words in the definition of a WBS: "A WBS is a family tree of all the project work ...." The reason teams must include as much of the work as possible in the WBS is simply that if a substantial piece of the work is left out, the schedule and budget estimates will be wrong. When the work is ultimately discovered as missing from the Project Plan during execution, time, resources, and money will have to be added, causing unpopular variances and missed expectations. Creating a WBS at the task level is the first real step in the detailed project planning effort.

Generally speaking, a project is composed of phases, such as design, development, test, deployment, and transition to operations and support. These phases can be broken down further into specific tasks for assignment to project team members. For each project phase and task, the question is whether that element can or should be broken down further to better define the project work to be accomplished. If the answer is yes, the element is broken into smaller pieces, each of which is similarly evaluated.

How detailed should the WBS be? It depends on how much management attention and control you, as the project manager, feel is needed to ensure the work is done. Break the project into too-small tasks and micromanagement will result. Tasks that are too comprehensive invite overlooking a critical element of the work that may delay the project if left unfinished. Good judgment is the key to a good work breakdown structure.

A WBS can be shown in either graphical or outline format. A graphical WBS looks a lot like an organization chart, as shown in Figure 3-3.

While it is a useful team-building exercise to create a WBS using sticky notes, most of the time a previous WBS will be available as a starting point. As a result, an outline view is usually the form the WBS takes. Figure 3-4 shows an outline view for building a new house on beautiful Beech Mountain, North Carolina. Notice that the WBS in Figure 3-4 has a column showing deliverables. Every task in the WBS

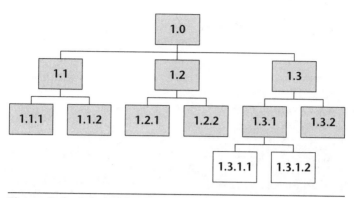

Figure 3-3. Graphical WBS

will have a corresponding deliverable—some tangible evidence of task completion. While not absolutely essential to include a deliverable for every task, it's a good idea to get in the practice of thinking this way. Later on, during the control phase of the project, you will need some measure to help you evaluate whether the work is being done on time and as specified. Having a measurable deliverable really helps!

A Word on Project Management Software

Notice I haven't mentioned using Microsoft *Project* or any other project management software. The reason I haven't mentioned it is simple: Most people don't have scheduling software, and many of those who do have it don't know how to use it effectively. Instead, the Just Enough approach uses software that nearly everyone has access to—Microsoft *Word*, *Excel*, *PowerPoint*, and *Outlook*. These aren't the only office suite packages available, but they are the ones I personally use, and they are widely available. You will find that all the templates in this book are *Word*, *Excel*, or *PowerPoint*. Furthermore, templates are fairly easy to create in these or similar programs, so feel free to create your own and use them regularly.

The template for creating the WBS and some of the other Project Plan elements is entitled the *Project Task Worksheet*. It's an *Excel* spreadsheet that starts with the

Task	Deliverable	Estimate	Person Assigned	Comp. Date
1.1 Clear site	Cleared site	6,000	Jones Chainsaws	Aug 15
1.2 Build foundation				
1.2.1 Excavate foundation	Graded site ready for footers	9,000	Smith Diggers	Sept 10
1.2.2 Pour footers	All footers in proper place	12,000	Jailors Construction	Sept 20
1.2.3 Lay concrete block	Concrete block walls erected	6,000	Blockbusters	Oct 1
1.3 Build house				
1.3.1 Frame house	Lumber framed house complete	37,000	Pyramid Builders	Oct 31
1.3.2 Put on roof	Installed roof, with Acme shingles, 544, green	21,000	Mountain Boys Bldrs	Nov 15
1.3.3 Install plumbing	Etc.	14,000	Barney	Dec 15
1.3.4 Install electrical	Etc.	19,000	Mountain Electric	Dec 21
n.n...				
1.9 Turn over keys	Completed house			July 14

Figure 3-4. WBS outline: Building Dream House on Beech Mountain

WBS and, as the project develops, includes other elements for resource assignments, planned task completion dates, actual completion dates, and comments. Figure 3-5 shows the blank template, and Figure 3-6 shows one filled out for a typical project.

Notice that in Figure 3-6 there are WBS tasks for project management. It's a good idea to add these tasks to the Project Plan so that you don't forget to do them! Plus, if your time is being charged to the project, you will need tasks to track your activities against the plan. Adding project management tasks also helps keep your efforts visible.

Task	Deliverable	By Whom	By When	Actual	Comment

Figure 3-5. Project task worksheet

Assign Resources

I stated earlier that forming the project team is the first and most important activity for the project manager. If you have followed the "script," you have held the kickoff meeting, and everyone is now motivated. It's time to begin in earnest the process of assigning or recommending resources to perform specific tasks in the WBS. When assigning resources, it is important to consider and resolve the following issues:

- Who and what do we need to make the project a success?
- Who is actually available?
- How can we make up the shortfall if resources aren't available when needed?
- Will resource constraints cause a schedule slip or budget overrun? (Any unresolved resource availability

Project Task Worksheet—Globus Offsite

Task	Deliverable	By Whom	By When	Actual	Comment
Project Mgt	Various				
Kickoff meeting	Meeting agenda	Sally Postitte	5/19/04		
Project Plan	Plan	Project team	5/20/04		
Status meetings	Status memos	Sally Postitte	Weekly		
Monitor and control the event	Adjustments as needed	Team	During event		
Capture lessons learned	Lessons-learned document	Sally and team	6/24/04		
Team celebration	Good time and lessons learned	Sally and team	6/25/04		
Finalize agenda	Agenda	Sally Postitte	5/21/04		
Arrange hotel	Contract	Jimmy Jones	5/25/04		
Finalize menu	Menu	Jimmy Jones	5/28/04		
Specify audio-visual equipt.	A/V list	Seiichi Nagao	6/1/04		
Get outside speaker	Contract	Bill McMurry	6/1/04		
Get outside trainer	Contract	Seth Godin	6/3/04		
Arrange entertainment	Contract	Bill McMurry	6/7/04		
Review Presentations	Approved presentations	Sally and Seth	6/7/04		
Dry run	Walk-through of event	Stake-holders	6/15/04		
Meeting setup & coordination	Rooms, catering, etc. set up	Team	6/17/04		
Meeting evaluation	Evaluations and summary	Seiichi Nagao	6/18–21/04		

Figure 3-6. Project task worksheet, completed

problems would eventually be reflected in one of the three triple constraints: schedule slippage, reduction in the technical content of the project, or cost overruns.)

Discuss shortfalls or bottlenecks with the project sponsor. When you have resolved the issues and have identified the team members who will do the work, add their names to the project task worksheet as shown in Figure 3-6. If the "by whom" is a vendor, enter that information instead of an individual's name.

Schedule the Work

Time—is there ever enough of it? Not in the world of projects. The project schedule is the "guts" of the Project Plan, and while it deals with time, it is affected by cost and technical elements of the project. The project manager is responsible for creating a *realistic* schedule, with the assistance of project team members.

Creating a project schedule consists of six fundamental steps:

1. Create a work breakdown structure to the task level.
2. Specify the person who will accomplish each task, as discussed earlier. Remember, most people cannot devote a full 8 hours each day to project work. Part of their time is lost to nonwork activities such as training, time off, coffee and smoke breaks, and so on. Another portion—sometimes sizable—is devoted to operational work. And your project is not the only one they are working on, so only a portion of their time is available for your project. Just be sure when people tell you it will take "X hours" to do a task, you know what they mean. Is that in view of everything else going on in their lives, or is that in a perfect world with no interruptions? In Chapter 4 we'll discuss this further. For now just make sure you understand the message being communicated.
3. Establish the dependencies between and among the tasks. In other words, decide when each task could begin and when it must begin, given the tasks that come beforehand. Also look at successor activities. Where does each task lead? What would be delayed if a task slipped? This is hard work, but it must be done to

develop a realistic schedule. If you are starting without a previous Project Plan as a guide, use sticky notes to show the relationships. If you have an earlier example, just add, delete, and change the tasks and relationships to reflect the current project. These efforts lead to identification of the critical path, discussed in Chapter 4.

4. In consultation with the responsible team member, determine the completion date for each task, keeping in mind the caveat from item 2, above.

5. Add task completion dates to the project task worksheet. Figure 3-6 shows a worksheet with the dates added. Remember to record all assumptions and issues that affect the schedule. You can embed them right in the spreadsheet using the "comments" feature. (Just right-click on the spreadsheet cell and click "Insert Comment.") This is important when discussing the rationale for the schedule with the sponsor and stakeholders.

6. Create the overall project schedule and completion date. With all tasks linked and assigned, and with completion dates established, the project end date can be calculated.

A Plan for Tracking Task Completions

To summarize where we are in planning, we have created the list of tasks—the WBS—and have, for each task, added the person who will perform the work ("by whom" on the spreadsheet) and the completion date ("by when"). We're making great progress, but we need a plan for how we will track completion dates later when work begins. This, and some advanced scheduling techniques, is covered in Chapter 4.

4

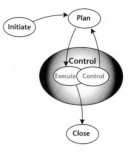

Advanced Planning Techniques

I N CHAPTER 3 WE TALKED ABOUT SOME OF THE BASICS OF PROJ-
ect planning. In this chapter we'll take it one step further
and present more advanced planning tools that will help
control the project. We'll also discuss why having a plan
for communicating is important and how to develop a
plan. We'll look at how to anticipate risks and develop a
plan to respond should such problems actually occur. And
we'll see how to control changes to the project scope so
that such changes do not erode the Project Plan and lead to
project failure.

Ways to Display the Project Schedule and Track Task Completions

The most successful project managers know exactly where
the project is with respect to the plan at all times. To make
the job of comparing actuals to the plan easier, three different views of the project schedule can be used: a simple calendar, a Gantt chart, or a network diagram. Often all three
views are used to give the project manager a different perspective.

Sun	Mon	Tue	Wed	Thur	Fri	Sat
		Enter project into JHSS		Verify price of materials		
	Get copy of signed proposal from CSM				Complete project plan	
		Identify lead trainer		Begin materials development		

Figure 4-1. Calendar view

The Calendar View

One simple yet effective way to track task completion dates is to use the calendar software most of us have on our computers. I personally use Microsoft *Outlook* when I am not using a project management scheduling application (Figure 4-1). *Outlook* allows me to add tasks to my calendar, share calendars with other team members, add pop-up reminders to make sure I keep my eye on key tasks coming up in the short run, and copy and paste information to other software for report preparation and e-mail. Immediately after nailing down the completion dates with team members, resolving constraints with the sponsor (and taking a look at risks—we'll discuss that below), I add the critical completion dates and milestones to my *Outlook* calendar and turn on the reminder function to give myself enough lead time to react if there is a problem.

This approach is so simple it's a wonder that more people don't use it. It works—try it!

The Gantt Chart

There are two other popular methods of portraying and tracking task completions: the *Gantt chart* and the *logic network* (also known as a *network diagram, PERT chart*, or *precedence diagram*). As a practical matter, these approaches can be used only if you are using project management software—unless you just happen to like constructing complex charts by hand! Still, no book on project management would be complete without touching on these tools.

Gantt charts—covered in every book and training course—are simply time-scaled, horizontal bar charts showing the start, finish, and duration of each task and its relationship to other tasks. While a calendar spreads the schedule over several pages, a Gantt chart shows the schedule on the same page as the WBS, and it provides a clear view of where the project is with respect to the planned schedule. This makes the Gantt an excellent briefing tool for periodic management reviews—even if you have to construct one periodically with presentation software. And of course, if you are using project management software, Gantt charts are automatically constructed once task dependencies and durations have been established. Figure 4-2 shows a generic Gantt chart.

Notice the schedule for tasks D1 and D2 in Figure 4-2. Both tasks have *float*, meaning their completion dates can slip by the amount shown without impacting the project completion dates. Task D1 can be delayed about a week and a half before it impacts task E1; and task D2 can be delayed two and a half weeks before it impacts E1.

Network Diagrams

Network diagrams show the logical relationships among tasks without a time scale. The great advantage of a network diagram is that it shows the *critical path* for the project—the sequence of tasks through the network on which any delay will cause a delay in the overall project completion date.

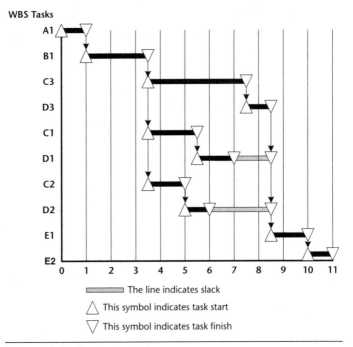

Figure 4-2. Gantt chart

Construction of a network diagram using sticky notes allows the team to visualize and portray the relationships among the tasks and to create the project completion date in a very logical and straightforward manner. Once a top-level network diagram has been constructed, the critical path can be shown on a Gantt chart if one is being used to brief the sponsor or other stakeholders. Critical tasks added to an *Outlook* calendar can be highlighted and tracked more closely than other tasks. (Be careful though—the critical path has a tendency to shift as slack is burned up on noncritical tasks.)

Network diagrams are difficult to maintain if you are not using project management software. For the initial planning session, however, they are nearly indispensable if the team is starting "from scratch." Figure 4-3 illustrates what a typical network diagram looks like.

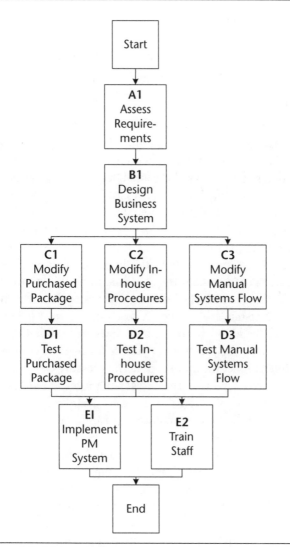

Figure 4-3. Network diagram

"Advanced" Scheduling

While *Just Enough Project Management* deals with the fundamentals that can be applied to all projects, large and small, I have been asked by several potential readers to add a few lines on more advanced scheduling considerations. In this section I'll cover a couple of real-world factors that tend to make most schedules overly optimistic—and what you can do to keep your schedules realistic.

Political Pressure

Thus far we have been discussing the project as though all members on the team, including the sponsor, other senior management, and other stakeholders, were purely rational. But that's not always the case. Unfortunately, despite our best efforts to put together a realistic plan, we frequently get "pushback" from management when we present the plan for approval. The sponsor may react emotionally, saying things like "Work smarter, not harder! Where's that can-do attitude? We've got to hold the line! Our competitors will beat us to market—cut the schedule in half!" I'm not denying that there are real market pressures out there, but much of the resistance we experience comes from a belief that there is "padding" in the plan somewhere and that the only way to keep the pressure on project teams is by condensing the initial schedule and keeping the pressure on.

What can you, as the project manager, do about this? My advice is to keep calm, take 10 deep breaths, and use the logic of the process to enter into an unemotional dialog with whoever is resisting. You have a powerful argument to support your plan—you've validated the requirement, assembled the experts, broken the requirement down into a logical work breakdown structure, used the WBS to establish task completion dates, and linked all the tasks together to produce a rational project completion. Now that's compelling! Couple this rational approach with the powerful competency of assertiveness, and you will convince the doubters that you and the team are right and those without the detailed knowledge are wrong.

What if, despite this approach, you still get resistance and pressure to reduce the schedule? Try inviting the person into a creative problem-solving session by pointing out that you and the team really believe that what you have come up with represents reality. But if you missed something, you would really like to know what it is and get the benefit of the experience and lessons learned. This dialog will result in one of three outcomes:

1. After going over the detailed plan, the person will support you and be convinced you know what you're doing.
2. You will adjust the plan based on the experience and helpful insights provided.
3. You will be told to "suck it up" and get to work. In this case, adjust the plan, document the conversation, and dust off your résumé because you will miss the project completion date. An old adage in project management is that if you agree to do something impossible—it's still impossible after you agree to it.

Project managers must stand up for what they believe to be realistic, even when confronted by the sponsor or other senior management.

The Natural Optimism of Project Managers

We project managers are an optimistic lot. Despite having learned some of our lessons the hard way, we still believe we can overcome all obstacles and achieve success. It might be a hero complex—but that's a topic for another book! Our can-do attitude is an asset in most cases, but it can get us into tight spots if we're not careful.

Because we are pressed for time, and perhaps because we are dealing with expert team members who provide us with their estimated completion dates, we use estimates when we put together the schedule. But when we rely on single-point estimates, we are denying the possibility that something could go wrong. There are models out there, however, that incorporate risk into the scheduling process.

Even the most basic scheduling models—for example, the *program evaluation and review technique* (PERT)— incorporate the possibility of worst-case and best-case scenarios. The widely known yet seldom used PERT model incorporates three estimates—optimistic, pessimistic, and most likely—to recognize that sometimes things go worse than expected, and sometimes you get lucky. Studies have shown that when a project manager uses a single estimate, it is closer to the optimistic than the worst-case (pessimistic) scenario. Figure 4-4 shows this graphically.

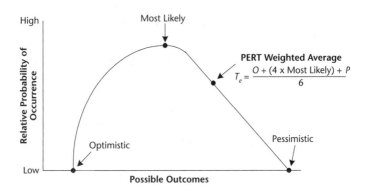

Figure 4-4. Distribution of project manager's schedule estimates

Notice in Figure 4-4 that the most-likely estimate is closer to the left-hand value, the optimistic estimate, than it is to the right side or pessimistic value. As a result, the overall project time estimate is more optimistic than it should be. You can check out this phenomenon on your real projects by taking a sample of 5 to 10 tasks and asking the person doing the work for the three estimates. You will consistently hear a most-likely estimate that is closer to the optimistic value than the pessimistic. What this means is that when you calculate a weighted average, the value of that average is "pulled" to the right by the pessimistic value. This results in a PERT, or weighted, value that is more pessimistic than the single-point, most-likely, estimate given to you initially. I like to think of this as a more realistic number, not pessimistic, given that so many projects exceed their planned completion dates.

For example, let's say one of your team members has told you that it will take her 10 days to complete a task. You enter that into the schedule with everyone else's estimates. Now let's say you decide to use the PERT approach, and you ask the person what the worst-case (pessimistic) estimate would be. She replies that for similar tasks in the past it has taken her as long as 20 days. When you ask her about the best case, she tells you she might be able to do it in 8 days if everything works out perfectly. Applying the PERT formula to these estimates yields an expected time (T_e) of 11.3 days, compared with the single-point estimate of 10 days—a difference of just 1.3 days. This doesn't sound like much, but even on a small project there will probably be 30 or 40 tasks. Let's say 15 of those tasks are on the critical path. Multiplying 1.3 days by 15 tasks equals 19.5 days! This is almost a complete work month! In a very real sense, your estimated completion date is understated by 1 month before you even begin the project. Now *that's* a sobering thought!

To keep this from happening to you, I encourage you to collect all three estimates for each task on your project, or at least the most critical tasks, calculate the expected times for these tasks, and use these values in your schedule rather than the single-point, most-likely values typically used. You can also add time to the schedule as a contingency against this phenomenon if you are unable to get three estimates from the busy people doing the work.

Statistics and Path Convergence

Many project managers don't understand statistics. As a result, they don't understand the probabilities associated with project success or failure. One way we can improve our chances of success is to use the PERT approach, discussed above. When we calculate expected times, we can also derive what is known as the *standard deviation*. That's a measure—a number—that represents how much time we would have to add to the schedule to increase the probability of success. But I'm getting ahead of myself.

First you need to know about a phenomenon known as *path convergence.*

The effects of path convergence occur when multiple paths converge in a network, such as that shown previously in the Gantt chart in Figure 4-2. In that project, tasks D1, D2, and D3 must all be finished on time or tasks E1 and E2 will not be able to start as planned. When this happens, we have to account for the joint probabilities. A *joint probability* occurs when two or more events are interdependent.

For example, see if you can answer this question: If you are 90 percent confident that all three tasks—D1, D2, and D3—will finish on time, what is the probability that tasks E1 and E2 can start on time? If you said 70 percent, you are correct. Any other answer is wrong. Here's the calculation: $0.9 \times 0.9 \times 0.9 = 0.72$. What this means is that we may think our success is 90 percent probable, but in fact , it is only 70 percent. And it gets worse. Let's say that you're also 90 percent confident that task E1 will go as planned. The joint probability is now $.72 \times .9 = .65$. And if the probability of task E2 is also .90, the probability that our project will come in on time is reduced to $.65 \times .9 = .58$. In other words, we have a 58 percent chance of successfully completing our project on time. So we're entering into our projects with drastically reduced probabilities of success, even when we're 90 percent confident that every task in the project will go exactly as planned.

The combination of single-point estimates and path convergences doom most schedules before we even get started—sobering news indeed. What can be done about it? The first step is to realize that these factors really do affect your project plans. The second is to determine how much time needs to be added to the schedule to raise the probability of completion back to a comfortable level. We could calculate the standard deviation—if we used the PERT approach—and add that to our expected times to improve our chances of success. Frankly, though, this is where most people's eyes glaze over—and don't even think about using this language with sponsors and other stakeholders.

So where does that leave us? Vulnerable, for sure. But we'll talk about risk management and adding management reserve to our project plans below. We must add reserves, or buffers, to be used at the disposal of the project manager to restore the odds. The only problem with this approach is that some people consider it padding. The simple fact is that these forces are at work on our projects, and we must plan accordingly to have a reasonable shot at success. And if people want to challenge you when you suggest creating this buffer, ask them what percentage of their projects come in on time. That should be enough evidence right there!

Project Budgeting

A wise friend of mine once said that all project cost overruns were estimating problems. And it's true—if we had perfect knowledge before a project began, we would produce the right estimates every time! In the real world that doesn't happen, but there are methods to help us establish fairly reliable cost estimates.

There are three levels of precision in project estimating, known as *top down*, *budgetary*, and *bottom up*.

Top-down budgeting: Recall that the Project Charter contained a cost estimate for the project. Where did this information come from? Probably a management estimate, based on previous experience, or perhaps it was the amount of a contract award, less overhead and profit. In either case, it was "the view from 30,000 feet." Top-down estimates by definition are not very precise and of limited use to project managers trying to control the project once it begins. Most top-down estimates are constraints—a limit to what the project manager can spend.

Budgetary estimating: When the project objective is clearly defined, categories of resources and expenses are known, and overhead information is available, budgetary estimating is appropriate. While this estimate is not as precise as a detailed, bottom-up estimate, often a budgetary estimate is "close enough" in the planning phase. If we know the "types" of labor we'll be using as well as other direct costs, such as materials and travel, and indirect costs, including labor and general and administrative overhead, we can develop reasonably accurate project budgets.

Bottom-up and/or detailed budgeting: The most precise estimate is derived by estimating the cost of each WBS task, summing all the estimates, then adding a reserve for risks to produce the project budget. Bottom-up estimating involves three simple steps:

1. **Calculate the total cost of each project task.** The team member assigned to each task should participate in estimating the cost of labor, materials, or other costs of performing the task.

2. **Sum all tasks to get the total project budget.** The project manager adds the costs for each task and produces the project budget.

3. **Add an amount for unforeseen contingencies.** (We'll talk about risk later.)

Once the bottom-up estimate is completed, compare the top-down estimate contained in the charter with the bottom-up estimate. Resolve discrepancies by discussing the differences with the project sponsor. Don't be bashful—part of your job is to manage expectations, and the earlier you address any discrepancies the better off you will be.

Risk Planning

Let's face it—not everything will go according to plan on the project, so it is prudent to consider the risks that typically occur in the project environment. Even on small projects, risk planning is important. Risks and planned mitigation strategies should be documented in the Project Plan. The project manager should ask himself or herself a simple question: "What could go wrong on this project?" At a minimum, consider the following questions when putting the plan together:

1. Are the customer's requirements well understood and documented?
2. Are costs and time estimates detailed or top down?
3. How likely is the project scope to change?
4. Will resources be dedicated to the project, or will they be available only on a part-time basis?
5. Will key resources be reassigned or otherwise lost to the project?
6. Will deadlines be pushed out by the customer or others?
7. Will the customer be responsive and meet key milestones?
8. Will we have technical problems?
9. Have we addressed the effects of single-point estimates and path convergences?

Formal risk assessment and planning are very important on large projects and covered in detail in training courses and books dedicated to major projects. But even on small projects we need to include risk planning as a formal step in our project planning efforts.

Risk can be defined as a function of three variables—an *event* that could disrupt the project, the *probability* that the event will happen, and the *impact* the event will have on the project if it does happen. The interaction of these three variables is shown in Figure 4-5.

If a risk event is likely and would have a catastrophic impact, it's obviously a high risk and must be dealt with. If an event is less likely and has a negligible impact, it's a low risk and can be accepted without further action. It's safe to say that all high-risk events and most moderate risks should be dealt with in the Project Plan.

Once risks are identified and analyzed, there are basically four ways to deal with them:

- **Avoid:** One sure fire way to avoid project risk is to not do the project. Sounds flip, but this decision should be made prior to the project being initiated by senior manage-

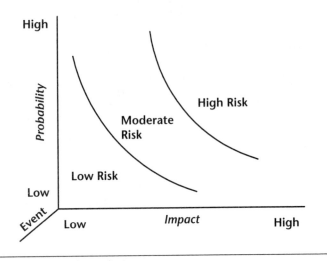

Figure 4-5. Risk Analysis

ment. Once the project has begun, the team might consider changing the Project Plan or technical approach to the work to eliminate high-technology solutions. Otherwise, avoidance is usually not an option.

- **Accept:** Acceptance literally means to take no action to reduce the probability or impact of the event. As Clint Eastwood says, "Do you feel lucky?" For example, if you get in your car and drive down an interstate highway at 70 miles an hour without your seatbelt on, you may literally accept the impact of your decision if you crash. Acceptance is generally not a wise choice for high-risk events.

- **Mitigate:** Mitigation means to take action to reduce the probability or impact of the risk. This is where the team will spend most of its time in risk planning. Ask yourself this question—what can you do right now during planning to reduce the probability or impact of the event? For example, a typical risk is the chance that a key resource will be pulled off the team when he or she is most needed. What can you do to mitigate this risk? You could outsource the task, or at least develop an outsourcing plan to be put into action should you get a sign the resource might leave. You could also develop a secondary resource through teaming to train someone else to fill in should the key resource leave. The objective is to lower the risk to an acceptable level so it won't kill or seriously damage the project. If nothing else, you can add contingency funds or time to the Project Plan "just in case."

- **Transfer:** Can you transfer or share this risk with another party? This strategy is normally used to respond to financial risk through insurance or contractual language.

It helps to have a template to focus the team's efforts when considering risk. Figure 4-6 shows a form I have used for years to help me identify and analyze risks and select an appropriate response strategy.

At the end of the risk planning session, the project manager selects the most appropriate responses and adjusts the triple constraint—time, cost, or technical approach and/or scope—to reflect the strategies and actions planned and taken.

Communication Planning

An essential element of every plan should be a discussion of the ways the team will communicate during the project and how status information will be communicated to project stakeholders. Despite our best intentions to communicate frequently with team members, once the project is underway, communications frequently break down. This results in surprises—and surprises on projects are not usually good! Poor communications result from two primary factors:

1. We get so busy that we forget or fail to keep the information flowing.
2. The project manager fails to plan for the exchange of information.

Project Information Project Name	Describe the event that could occur.
Project Manager/Phone	
Task	
WBS # of Task	
High	

	Describe the significant impact on the project if this occurs
Probability of Occurrence	
	Describe the probability of the event occurring.

Low Impact High	

For each response strategy below, discuss the advantages and disadvantages, and the n select the response that fits the situation.

	Risk Responses			
Strategy	**Avoid**	**Accept**	**Mitigate**	**Transfer**
Advantages				
Disadvantages				
Order of Preference				

Figure 4-6. Risk Management Template

These two causes are linked. If the Project Plan includes the communication requirements and expectations of the team, chances are information will flow and there will be fewer surprises.

Communicating in a project environment is not easy. The number of communication links multiplies exponentially as the number of team members grows, as shown below:

Number of communication channels in a network:

$$\frac{n\,(n-1)}{2}$$

For example, with five team members there are

$$\frac{5\,(5-1)}{2} = 10 \text{ channels}$$

And with seven members there are

$$\frac{7\,(7-1)}{2} = 21 \text{ channels!}$$

Clearly, the project manager must make it one of his or her highest priorities to plan and continue to carry out project communications.

The Project Plan should always include a paragraph or two describing the following elements:

- Who needs information?
- Why do they need it?
- What do they need?
- When do they need it?
- What form should the communication take?
- When should the project team meet to discuss status, problems, and so on?

Every project will be slightly different, but in general, team members communicate project status to the project manager on a weekly basis, the project manager consolidates it, assesses the overall status of the project, and passes that along to the sponsor and customer, along with any work-arounds to overcome setbacks. Here are some tried-and-true guidelines:

- Communicate frequently with team members, the sponsor, and the customer.
- Review your ideas, drafts, and plans with them.

- Get their approval on pending changes.
- Get their approval on final deliverables.
- Establish a "continuing dialogue" with the team.

Following these guidelines should keep everyone informed and committed to the project objectives.

As for the form routine status reports should take, it's hard to beat a simple memo or e-mail. Figure 4-7 shows an example of a status report using a simple memo format. For a slightly more formal progress report, consider using the format shown in Figure 4-8.

Project Status Memo

To: Curtis Cook
From: Shamika Reyes
CC: Robert Seals
Re: New Telephone Equipment Project Status Report
Date: 12-4-04

Accomplishments this week:
1. Put together a document containing all training requirements along with description of each one.
2. Identified potential printers and pricing.
3. Began work on brochure to inform employees of new system.

Issues needing action:
1. Graphics warns of slow turnaround due to overload in their area.

Overall status of project: Green

Figure 4-7. Simple Project Status Memo

Change Control Process

Managing changes during a project is one of the most important aspects of project management. *Scope creep*—unconstrained scope expansion—can drive the project schedule and budget over the approved baseline.

WEEKLY STATUS REPORT

To: From: Project Name: For Week Ending:	
ACTIVITIES AND ACCOMPLISHMENTS THIS WEEK	List the week's activities and accomplishments for this project. Refer to WBS when reporting accomplishments, plans, and issues. 1. _____ 2. _____ 3. _____
PLANS FOR WEEK ENDING _____	State the next week's objectives and significant activity for this project. 1. _____ 2. _____ 3. _____
CHANGES TO TARGET DATES	List any new, changed, or significant target dates.

Task	Revised Target Date

ASSUMPTIONS	List any assumptions.
ISSUES	List any issues (new or open) that require an action plan.
RISKS	List any new or continuing risks associated with the project.

Figure 4-8. Weekly Project Status Memo

Change control is really a mindset. It says that nothing in the approved Project Plan can change without the involvement of the project manager. At a minimum, the change control process should include the following:

1. All changes must be submitted to the project manager on a change request form or e-mail.
2. Changes are logged in using a simple spreadsheet.
3. The team assesses the impact of the change on schedule, budget, and specifications.
4. The impact is discussed with the requester. (Often the change request is withdrawn when the impact is known.)
5. The proposed change is discussed with the sponsor and customer.
6. The change is either approved or disapproved, and the requestor is notified of the decision. (Make sure everyone understands who can approve changes before starting the project.)
7. Stakeholders are notified of the change.
8. The change is incorporated into the Project Plan and deliverables.

On small projects change requests can be submitted via e-mail, but on larger, more complex projects, a *change request template* should be used, such as the one shown in Figure 4-9.

At first glance the change control process looks cumbersome, but it is really very simple. It does require a level of rigor some organizations are not used to and may not accept. You and senior management must be the judge of how much process is just enough to control changes in your organization.

Approval of the Project Plan

After all the elements of the plan have been completed, the project manager and team review the entire plan to ensure that it is internally consistent. This review ensures that all significant plan elements have been integrated and that the team has one source of information it can use to help

DOCUMENT PREPARATION INFORMATION			
Project Name	Prepared by	Date Prepared	Project ID

PROPOSED CHANGE

CHANGE DESCRIPTION Define the desired change in sufficient detail to enable the team to evaluate it. Identify all WBS elements affected by the change.

REASON FOR CHANGE Describe why this change is necessary or desirable.

SCHEDULE AND BUDGET IMPACT State the effect on the project schedule and cost to complete this change. Include the duration and cost of the specific change as well as overall impact, if known.

ASSUMPTIONS List any business and technical assumptions.

AUTHORIZATION — PROJECT MANAGER			
Name (print)	Signature	Phone	Date

AUTHORIZATION — PROJECT SPONSOR			
Name (print)	Signature	Phone	Date

Figure 4-9. Change Request Template

control the project once work begins. This is a crucial step in the project management life cycle. Up until this moment, not much time or money has been spent. Once the plan has been approved, however, resources begin charging their time to the project, and costs begin to accumulate rapidly. Without an approved baseline, objective control of technical, cost, and schedule performance will be difficult, if not impossible.

Transition to Control Phase

Approval of the Project Plan signifies the end of the planning phase and the start of the physical effort and the control phase of the project life cycle. This is a good time to take the team out for a little celebration! After this, the pressure will continue to mount on the team to keep the project going according to the plan.

You'll recall the planning phase started with a lot of hoopla. You conducted a kickoff meeting, got the sponsor to attend, and got the team motivated. While there is no similar formal meeting to launch implementation and control, it's a good idea to get the team together with the sponsor to formalize the plan approval and to get a "booster shot" from the sponsor as work begins.

5

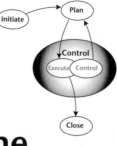

Controlling the Project

NOW FOR THE HARD PART. THE PROJECT IS UNDER WAY, and things are happening. Tasks are being worked on, problems arise, changes occur. What seemed clear and manageable is now becoming blurred and hard to get our arms around. We are deluged with information— task completions, task delays, issues needing attention, and meetings to attend. Our challenge is to stay in CONTROL.

Control Activities

During the control phase of the project, the project team carries out the project according to the baselined Project Plan. Following the work breakdown structure, the schedule, and other Project Plan elements, the team works to achieve project milestones and to meet the project objectives. The project manager deals with changes to the project or deviations from the plan as they occur during project execution.

The activities in this phase are actually carried out in parallel rather than sequentially. The project manager must control these activities and ensure that they focus on the completion of the project according to its performance goals.

The specific activities the project manager performs during this phase are shown in Figure 5-1. We'll discuss each one in turn.

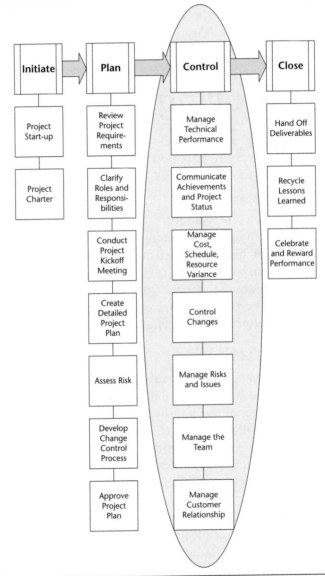

Figure 5-1. Process block diagram with the control steps highlighted

Manage Technical Performance

The objective of most projects is to provide a solution to a business need. The project manager must ensure that technical progress, as well as progress in other areas, is being made toward the objectives. All the planning, execution, and control processes are put in place for one reason—to satisfy the stated requirements in the Project Charter. Whether that performance results in a physical product or service, it forms the very basis for the existence of the project.

Your job as the project manager, even if you are performing some of the technical work yourself, is to monitor all technical work being performed and evaluate progress relative to the Project Plan. Your source of information, of course, is the project team. We'll discuss team management later, but it is obvious that without a high level of trust and respect between the project manager and the team, information flowing to the project manager on the status of the technical work will be distorted.

Based on the information you receive, you will initiate corrective action for any variances that appear. The form that might take is discussed below. You will also be monitoring change activity on technical tasks, enforcing the change control process, and incorporating changes into the plan as approved by the sponsor. Constant communication on technical progress among all team members, including the customer, is of paramount importance.

Clearly the project manager cannot be a mere project administrator and be involved in any meaningful relationship with the more technically oriented team members. While many scholars and practitioners insist that the project manager does not need to be schooled in the technology involved in the project, for small projects technical knowledge is a must. However, the larger the project, the less technical knowledge is required. In fact, on major projects attempts on the part of the project manager to involve himself or herself in the technical aspects of the project is probably a mistake. To put it into plain terms, if the project manager is over in aisle 9 stocking the shelves, who is watching the cash register and minding the store? The project could spin out of control in one technical area while the project manager is deeply involved in his or her favorite technology. The larger the project, the more the project manager needs to focus on leading the project team.

Communicate Achievements and Project Status

Are you meeting the expectations of the customer and sponsor? Don't assume you are—communicate! Believe it or not, most people forget to do this. They get so busy doing the work and managing the project—translated as fighting fires—they neglect this very important aspect of project control. Regular status reports and short visits help ensure that you are meeting expectations. Frequent communication also helps you build your informal influence with the team and gives the sponsor the information he or she needs to report progress and problems to his or her bosses. Project status memos really help.

The form and frequency of team meetings, status reports from team members to you, the project manager, and status reports to the sponsor and other stakeholders— all of this should have been worked out and explicitly set forth in the Project Plan. If it wasn't, you will have problems at this point getting everyone "on the same page" with respect to the exchange of project information. But if the plan didn't include this information, now is the time to establish the protocols you will use for the rest of the project. It's a good idea to amend the plan with this information so you will not have to fight this issue repeatedly later in the project when things heat up.

Let's assume you did it right and documented communication requirements and exchanges in the Project Plan. All you have to do at this point is follow the plan. Use the selected project status report form or forms to gather information from the team to be passed along to the sponsor and other stakeholders.

To Meet or Not to Meet—That Is the Question

In the Project Plan, you may have made a general comment to the effect that the team would meet "as necessary" to resolve problems in addition to attending the customary weekly status meeting or conference call. But as a practical matter, when should the team physically meet? On one hand, you want to avoid ritual meetings that serve no useful purpose, while on the other hand, you want to meet often enough to maintain team identity and spirit. Follow these general guidelines to strike the right balance:

- Meet one on one to resolve individual problems.
- Meet as a group to discuss issues of joint concern and get input from team members.

The most frequent type of meeting is the project status meeting. These meetings offer the project manager the opportunity to solicit feedback, status, information, and ideas from the team on various aspects of the project. They provide team members an opportunity to interact with one another.

As the project manager, you are responsible for planning and conducting the meetings and for ensuring that meeting objectives are stated and achieved. The following steps will help you hold productive meetings:

1. Prepare an agenda (use the kickoff meeting agenda as an example) stating the purpose of the meeting, its expected duration, a list of attendees, and so on.
2. Notify attendees at least 1 week in advance of each project status meeting.
3. Ensure that the meeting covers the topics on the agenda.
4. Document action items and other decisions arising from the meeting.

5. Distribute the meeting minutes to all invitees (not just attendees).

6. Ensure that action items, along with the individual responsible for taking action, are recorded on the agenda for the next scheduled project status meeting.

Manage Cost, Schedule, and Resource Variances

Three key performance measurements for the project manager, in addition to technical performance, are cost variance, schedule variance, and resource use. Keep a close eye on these and you will have your finger on the pulse of the project.

Using status information provided by the team, you will become aware of cost and schedule variances against the plan and any resource constraints that are threatening progress. Based on the nature of the problem and situation and in collaboration with the team, your job is to formulate and take action to correct the problem and bring the project back into line. If you can't solve the problem yourself, escalate the issue to the sponsor, along with your recommended corrective action.

In some cases the Project Plan may have to be revised if the project budget, schedule, or resource plan cannot be maintained. If so, the project manager works closely with the sponsor and customer to revise the plan, keep the team motivated, and continue to make progress against the revised plan.

There are as many specific corrective actions for specific project problems as there are problems themselves, so a detailed list of how to "fix" a project that is out of control is nearly impossible, given the scope of this book. There are some general approaches that you might want to consider, however, to help you manage and recover from variances:

- Apply more or different resources to tasks that are behind schedule, especially those on the critical path.

Keep in mind, however, that throwing resources at a task that is behind schedule doesn't usually fix the problem.

- Reconfigure the Project Plan so that tasks are accomplished in a different sequence or in parallel. Although risk increases when tasks are performed in parallel, at times this action does result in acceleration of the work. Resources have to be available to do these tasks, however, and it has been my experience that resources are not usually available when you need them to fast-track the project in this way.

- Reallocate resources among projects (take resources from a low-priority project). If you are lucky enough to work in an organization that prioritizes its projects according to their contribution to strategic objectives, you can make a case for "robbing Peter to pay Paul." If you can show that your higher-priority project will suffer because of lack of resources and that resources are available on a less critical project, you may be able to convince the sponsor to take action. This won't make you popular with the project manager of the lower-priority project, but if that project's plan is adjusted for the loss of the resource, the project manager will not be penalized for failing to meet objectives.

- Change or reduce the scope of work (subject to agreement by the customer). Unfortunately, we frequently are forced to this last and least desirable alternative. If the schedule is the highest-priority objective, scope will often be reduced to preserve the completion date. Most often the scope that is lopped off becomes the starting point for a follow-up project for the next generation or release of the product.

Naturally some of these actions will increase cost. If more resources are added to a task that is behind schedule, that usually results in overtime, cost of an outside consultant, or just application of more labor hours to get the job done. The project manager will have to discuss these impacts with the sponsor and customer before taking action.

Remember our project task worksheet? It's time to update the form with actual completion dates, replanned dates, and comments reflecting reasons for variance. Figure 5-2 shows a partially updated project task worksheet to reflect actual progress on a few tasks.

PROJECT TASK WORKSHEET—GLOBUS OFFSITE					As of 6/4/04
Task	**Deliverable**	**By Whom**	**By When**	**Actual**	**Comment**
Project Mgt.	Various				
Kickoff meeting	Meeting agenda	Sally Postitte	5/19/04	5/19/04	
Project Plan	Plan	Project team	5/20/04	5/20/04	
Status meetings	Status memos	Sally Postitte	Weekly		
Monitor and control the event	Attachments as needed	Team	During event		
Capture lessons learned	Lessons-learned document	Sally and team	6/24/04		
Team celebration	Good time and lessons learned	Sally and team	6/25/04		
Finalize agenda	Agenda	Sally Postitte	5/21/04	5/23/04	Sally out sick first two days
Arrange hotel	Contract	Jimmy Jones	5/25/04	5/25/04	
Finalize menu	Menu	Jimmy Jones	5/28/04	5/31/04	Team couldn't agree on menu—delayed decision over weekend
Specify audio-visual equipt.	A/V list	Seiichi Nagao	6/1/04	6/4/04	Seiichi pulled off project due to higher priorities

Figure 5-2. Updated project task worksheet (continued on next page)

PROJECT TASK WORKSHEET—GLOBUS OFFSITE				As of 6/4/04	
Task	Deliverable	By Whom	By When	Actual	Comment
Get outside speaker	Contract	Bill McMurry	6/1/04		
Get outside trainer	Contract	Seth Godin	6/3/04		
Arrange entertainment	Contract	Bill McMurry	6/7/04		
Review presentations	Approved presentations	Sally and Seth	6/7/04		
Dry run	Walk-through of event	Stake-holders	6/15/04		
Meeting setup and coordination	Rooms, catering, etc. setup	Team	6/17/04		
Meeting evaluation	Evaluation and summary	Seiichi Nagao	6/18–21/04		

Figure 5-2. Updated project task worksheet (continued)

Control Changes

Every sizable project will experience changes in technical design, schedule, estimated costs, resources, or other project aspects. However, if those changes are not carefully and rigorously controlled, the project can easily get out of control, as depicted in Figure 5-3.

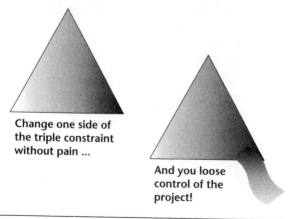

Change one side of the triple constraint without pain ...

And you loose control of the project!

Figure 5-3. Change control

The project manager is responsible for implementing and, with the sponsor's help, enforcing the change control process that was specified in the Project Plan to ensure that the project does not suffer the catastrophic consequences of scope creep. Remember, the project scope is defined as the work content—all the activities and deliverables—included in the project. Scope creep occurs when changes to the scope occur that the project manager is not aware of and that erode the budget and schedule without his or her knowledge or control. Just to review, these are the essential steps in the change control process to minimize scope creep:

1. Change request submitted.
2. Change request logged in.
3. Impact on Project Plan assessed.
4. Sponsor approves or rejects.
5. Documentation is changed if approved, and team is informed.

A rigorous process will help make sure that changes to the project are identified, documented, and processed properly. This ensures that project documentation is updated to reflect changes, that budgets or schedules are adjusted appropriately, and that ultimately the deliverables resulting from the project meet customer expectations. Without change control—trust me—chaos will reign, and the project will be in danger of failing or at least overrunning the budget and schedule. Let me give you an example.

My wife used to work for an architect in Columbus, Ohio. When she joined the firm, she was handed a thick folder of documentation that had been "collected" on a major retirement community construction project the firm had designed and performed construction oversight on. Many of the documents made reference to changes that had been made to the design during construction of the facility. Her responsibility was to negotiate the net effect of these changes on the contract with the construction prime contractor and settle any disputes.

She entered into a dialogue with the contractor and found dozens of undocumented changes that had been directed by her firm's on-site construction manager. None of these had gone through a change control process; therefore the impact on the construction budget and schedule had never been assessed. The construction contractor, however, had kept records of the time, date, and nature of the changes directed and was able to prove a substantial cost and schedule impact. The bottom line was that all of the profit my wife's firm planned to make on the project was eaten up by unauthorized changes. This could have been avoided simply by following the commonsense change control process discussed earlier. Remember the motto, "A deal is a deal; extras cost extra." It's that simple.

Manage Risks and Issues

Much of the change activity on projects is really about risk events that are occurring. If the team did a good job of brainstorming risks and response strategies, many of these events will have been anticipated and responses will be ready for implementation. There will be fewer surprises and less fire fighting. Even with the most prescient project team, however, some unknowns will creep into the project. For that reason, risk and issues management is an ongoing activity.

What's the difference between a risk and an issue? We've already discussed risk extensively in Chapter 4, but to review, *risks* are events that could undermine or destroy the project—something that could really hurt you. We can anticipate risk; therefore, during Project Planning the team addresses potential risks and planned responses and documents the Project Plan. As the project unfolds, risk is addressed on a continuing basis and new risks are handled in much the same way as they were during planning. As risk events occur, the appropriate response is implemented.

Issues, on the other hand, are things that just need to be addressed as they come up during the project. They are tracked on a simple spreadsheet called an *issues log*. (No need for a template—it's that simple.) Left unresolved, they could escalate into problems that could have a negative impact on the project. Issues are assigned to someone for resolution and tracked at project status meetings or more frequently, depending on the urgency.

For risks and issues, project managers with a flexible, proactive attitude are better equipped to handle bad news when it arrives—as it inevitably will sooner or later. As the saying goes, Murphy is alive and well and will visit your project—you just don't know when. Continue to involve the team in risk and issues management. Discuss risks, issues, and changes at every team meeting to minimize the number of surprises. Team members are closest to the work being performed and are, therefore, best equipped to identify, analyze, and respond to risks that emerge during the course of the project.

One final reminder—continue to use the risk management template provided earlier to focus on the three elements that make up risk: the event itself, its probability, and the impact if it occurs. Respond to moderate and high risks and accept the rest. And don't get bogged down in formality here. Envision yourself as fast, fleet-afoot, creative, and agile. (Who wouldn't want to be described this way?) Remember, your job during the control phase is to keep the project on track. This takes constant vigilance, especially as events and issues occur that delay the project or send it over budget.

Manage the Project Team

Project management is about dealing with other human beings on a personal level, helping the team achieve project objectives while helping individuals achieve their professional and personal goals. And the smaller the project, the more difficult it is, due to the part-time nature of project teams! This is a tough job—one that is not intuitive in many cases.

When we described the planning phase, we discussed the importance of selecting the right resources for the project. There is more to selecting the right person for the job than evaluating his or her technical expertise. It's a good idea to discuss how the project can contribute to the professional and personal goals of the individuals in addition to the technical competence. When project, professional, and personal goals are all aligned, project management seems easy. When there's a disconnect, it's difficult to get people to put their hearts and minds into the project work.

Regardless of the size of the project or whether the team is full time or part time on your project, managing the team is one of the most crucial activities a project manager performs. When the team gets busy and problems occur, teams can fragment—with a disastrous impact on the project. Project team management involves leadership, motivation, team building, conflict resolution, decision making, and constant communication with the team.

The scope of this book restricts how much attention we can give to leadership—and, believe me, there is much that we all need to know when we set out to convince others to *want* to do what we think is the right thing to do. A good source for more information on the leadership dimension is James P. Lewis' *Project Leadership*. (See the Further Reading section.) We will, however, take a look at three important aspects of managing teams—managing conflict, establishing expectations through team charters, and rewarding outstanding performance.

Managing Conflict

One of the project manager's less pleasant but most important tasks is to manage conflict. Not enough conflict and the team may stagnate. Too much and the team is torn apart. One conceptually simple model for dealing with conflict is shown in Figure 5-4. There are five approaches to managing conflict, each of which is appropriate in a different situation. In the model below, the vertical axis deals

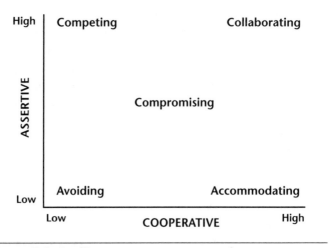

Figure 5-4. Conflict management approaches

with assertiveness, also known as "getting your way," while the horizontal represents cooperation, otherwise known as the other party "getting its way."

Competing. The competing approach is usually called *win-lose,* but it doesn't have to be a losing proposition for either party. The project manager is assertive about the issue in question, pushing for his or her solution with little cooperation or involvement with the other party. When might this be appropriate? When time is of the essence, such as in natural disasters or war. As long as the team is aware of and supports this approach when the conditions warrant, the project manager is in the clear. Overreliance on the competing approach will lead to charges that the project manager is an autocrat—seldom a good thing.

Accommodating. At the opposite extreme is accommodating. This occurs when the project manager cooperates fully with the other party by adopting his or her solution. This approach is appropriate when the other party is the expert and their solution is better. It is also politically appropriate when the issue is of little importance to the project manager but seems important to the other party. As the saying goes, you don't have to win every battle to win the war. It's a good idea to allow the other party to save face, even when you could dominate every decision.

Avoiding. When avoiding, both parties withdraw from the conflict. As a long-term strategy, avoiding doesn't work. Whoever said "Ignore it and it will go away" was not a project manager! As a short-term strategy, however, it is appropriate when the atmosphere is emotionally charged. If you feel like jumping up and smacking the person on the other side of the table, it's time to put the issue on the back burner for a while to let things cool down. In the political arena, senators often table an issue for a short period to allow tempers to cool and additional information to be collected.

Collaborating. In this strategy, also known as *problem solving*, both parties get nearly everything on their agendas by confronting the issues head-on. Facts and feelings are laid on the table and dealt with openly. This strategy is beautiful—but requires a high degree of trust between the parties and a real belief that neither party will take advantage of the other's honesty. On small projects this is possible, but on larger ones, my experience has been that you need to be careful to not divulge all your issues until you are absolutely sure of the other party's integrity.

Compromising. Welcome to the real world! The most effective way to resolve most conflicts is through negotiation—the process of give and take. In compromising, both parties are satisfied that their needs have been met and both can support the decision or resolution of the issue. Not that compromise is easy or even desirable in some cases, as discussed above. But through skillful negotiating—which by the way can be learned—almost anyone can achieve his or her objectives. Is compromise always the right approach? No, as we have discussed. Consensus decision making—a form of the compromise approach—takes more time than the competing or accommodating approaches. If time is not available but the team believes it is involved in a consensus process, problems will arise if the project manager "gets in a bind" and makes a unilateral decision.

Team Charter. One important aspect of any approach you take is the team's support when you use that approach. How can you be assured that you have this support? One way is to develop a team charter the first time you meet for project planning.

Team charter is another term for the rules of engagement your team will follow when meeting for any reason. Elements of a team charter include the following:

- **Etiquette:** The team should decide the rules for arriving on time, staying for the whole meeting, allowing others to speak without interrupting, using profanity, missing meetings, being disruptive, and so on. Sound like kindergarten? Well, ... some projects I've been on have needed this level of detail on acceptable behavior. You be the judge on how much is enough for your team.

- **Decision making and conflict resolution:** Which of the models discussed above for making decisions and resolving conflict will the team use? This should be clearly stated in the team charter.

- **Who can call a meeting?** Is the project manager the only person authorized to call a meeting? This is usually the case, but for more mature teams using a collaborative decision-making approach, any core team member can call a meeting and other team members are expected to respect that request.

Those are just a few elements of a team charter. Even if you don't use a formal charter, it's always a good idea to discuss these things with the team to avoid conflict, resentment, and the resultant loss of effectiveness. And once a team establishes its own rules of engagement, it's up to the project manager—and the team—to enforce those rules when the going gets tough later in the project.

Rewarding Excellence

The project manager is also responsible for making sure stellar performance is recognized and that team members receive appropriate rewards for doing a good job. When you take good care of people, they will take care of you—and you might be surprised at how easy it is to motivate most project team members. We're going to defer discussing rewards and celebrations until the next chapter on project closing.

Manage the Customer Relationship

All projects begin and end with the customer. There are two objectives in customer relationship management. One is to establish a good working relationship and level of trust with the customer, while the other is to obtain customer signoff on the project deliverables.

Customer Relationship

Throughout the life of a project, the project manager is responsible for keeping the customer informed and satisfied. In this effort the project manager should be given the full support of all levels of management within the organization. In focusing on the customer, the project manager performs the following duties:

- Understands the customer's requirements
- Develops project objectives that address the customer's requirements—and validates these with the customer before starting work
- During project planning, plans for customer involvement, communication, and management of expectations
- Seeks the customer's approval of the Project Plan and subsequent changes to the plan during execution

A number of methods are available for maintaining customer focus, and they may seem to be simply common sense to successful project managers. Still, they bear repeating:

- **Get to know the client and establish a good relationship.** Take advantage of the opportunity to discuss the customer's needs and expectations. Learn about the customer's organization by reading the business press, searching the Internet, or just asking.
- **Establish a continuous dialogue with the customer.** This goes beyond the typical progress report or project status meeting. It literally means to establish personal, two-way communications with the customer and as many key staff on the customer's team as possible. Listen to what the customer says with attention and focus. Beyond the obvious advantage of building a better relationship, another advantage of this level of involvement is that the project manager can learn about opportunities for additional services and product sales.
- **Cultivate the relationship.** A one-to-one professional relationship with the customer's project manager or point of contact is the minimum requirement. The relationship can go much further, developing into a relationship of trust and good feelings between one organization and another.

Customer Signoff

Signoff by the customer signals the conclusion of the project to many of the stakeholders. Of course, we project managers know there are other administrative and management duties still to be performed, but signoff is the major objective, and without it, we don't get paid!

Naturally, for us to obtain signoff, the customer has to be satisfied that we have met the project requirements. If we have done a good job with maintaining the customer relationship and managing changes during the project, the customer's expectations will have been met and formal signoff will be easy. If we haven't, chances are there will be unmet expectations and hard feelings. Let's assume we have a good relationship and that the deliverable matches what the customer expects to see.

At this point, just make sure that all project requirements have been satisfied and that any open issues have been documented and assigned for follow-up. Review any project documents, specifications, list of deliverables, and contractual documents, if any, to verify that all commitments have been met. Once this review has been completed, prepare a formal signoff document for the customer's signature. This acceptance document should be in writing because it forms the basis for submitting the invoice to the customer for the work performed.

Transition to Project Closing Phase

The project is nearly finished! The customer is satisfied and wants to continue to do business with you! Now you're ready to finish up the project, reward the team, and recycle those hard-won lessons learned for use by future teams. All this is covered in the next exciting chapter on closing the project.

6

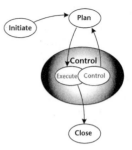

Closing the Project

PROJECT CLOSE IS THE LAST PHASE OF THE PROJECT LIFE cycle. The project is considered complete when the project manager has verified that all objectives have been met and the customer has accepted the deliverables—but that's not all. Remember the Thanksgiving project? The project manager still has a few "chores" to do after the project has apparently been completed, as shown in Figure 6-1.

Project close activities are always important, regardless of the size of the project, yet projects are seldom closed out correctly. This is due primarily to the fact that the people who did the work may have already been assigned to other projects. That is just the nature of working in a matrix with part-time team members. But it's also true that many project managers either don't know what to do to close a project properly or just don't take the time due to the crush of other work.

When we don't complete projects the right way, we miss a golden opportunity to improve, and improvement is one of the most important human motivators—we all want to get better at what we do. Project close is a powerful mechanism for improvement. Regardless of whether a project hit the mark or missed it in some way, it contains the seeds of suc-

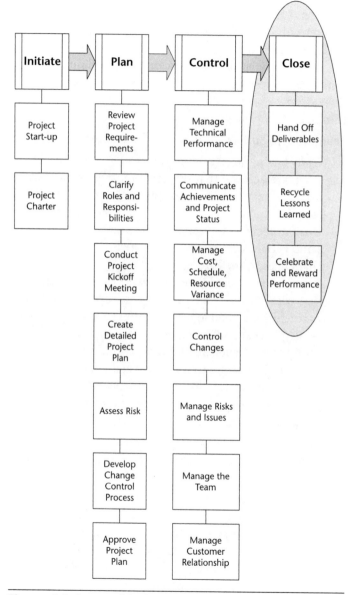

Figure 6-1. Process block diagram with the closing steps highlighted

cess for future projects. What did we do right? What did we do wrong? How can we benefit from what we learned? This chapter will equip you with some useful tools to help you focus on these questions.

Before looking at the "how to" of closing a project, it might be interesting to look at it from the opposite perspective. What happens when we *don't* close projects? Several things, and they are all negative.

Team Morale Suffers. This occurs for two reasons:

- First, having a clear objective and a sense of closure when we achieve that objective motivates most of us. If the project is not closed properly but is allowed to languish and die a slow death, team members drift off without feeling that sense of closure. As a result, these same people will be less motivated to take on project challenges in the future.

- Second, most people are motivated by the recognition that comes from management and peers as a result of having done a good job. Motivation theorists call these *esteem needs,* and, based on my experience, most project team members are operating at this level. When we don't close out our projects, we usually fail to recognize team members for their performance. They don't get their esteem needs met, and we lose a great opportunity.

Costs Mount Up. The second problem that results from not closing the project is in the area of cost. Open projects are magnets for costs, leading to cost overruns. This occurs for a couple of reasons:

- Team members who are still loosely assigned to the project continue to "tweak" the deliverable, running up costs. These improvements should really be the front end of a new project for the "new, improved" version of the product, but since the old project is still technically alive, that work continues. Unfortunately the customer has already accepted the deliverable, so the costs of the improvements are not reimbursed.

- In many organizations the Project Charter contains a billing code against which team members charge their time. Once the deliverable is handed over to the customer, the project manager should close the project account. Otherwise, the project will be a magnet for odds and ends that are only peripherally related to the project. There is also a possibility that someone might bill his or her time against the open project account rather than record it as overhead—the kiss of death in a services organization.

Lessons That Were Learned Are Lost. Finally, if a project is not closed, lessons learned will not be collected to help future project teams. Lessons learned are one of the primary means through which we improve our performance. Unless the project is properly closed, chances are that these lessons will be lost—and that is a real waste.

Now that we've seen the downside of not closing a project properly, let's turn our attention to how to do it right. Begin by asking yourself the four questions posed below. If you answer these questions satisfactorily, chances are you will bring your project to a successful completion.

- Were expectations met?
- Were objectives accomplished?
- Did we learn anything?
- Have we communicated thanks and acknowledgment?

Remember, you and the sponsor specified success and completion criteria at the initiation stage, so you should know if the objectives were accomplished!

A Model for Closing a Project

Let's give project close some structure by looking at it as a three-step model, as shown in Figure 6-2.

Hand Off

You'll recall we discussed customer signoff as the last activity in the control phase of the project, so at this point you're

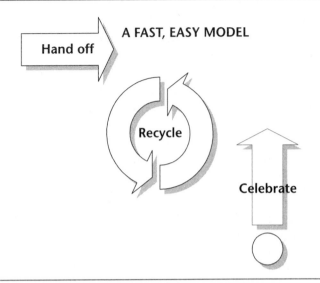

Figure 6-2. Project Close Model

just making sure that the formal acceptance document has been signed and returned by the customer. For internal customers, such as a business unit acting as the customer for an information technology project, you may not get formal, written acceptance. In this case, just validate the items below in much the same manner as you would for an external customer.

Obtain Acceptance and Approval of the End Result. With a signature if possible, otherwise e-mail at a minimum.

Evaluate How Well Expectations Were Met. As a practical matter, how can you measure satisfaction? Many organizations use a customer satisfaction survey, with what's known as a *Likert scale,* to measure satisfaction on a scale of, say, 1 to 7. If you have maintained a good customer relationship throughout the project as discussed in Chapter 5, you will know whether the customer is satisfied with the end result.

Nail Down Loose Ends. This is a catchall category to take care of all the little details that need attention at the end of a project. Figure 6-3 shows a project closeout checklist that is probably much more than you will need to close out most of your projects. But I think it's better to have too much detail in this case than too little.

Recycle

Here we deal with capturing lessons learned and putting them to use to help future project teams.

Capture Lessons Learned. In hindsight, every project could have been managed a little differently, perhaps a little better, had the project manager and team had more experience with the specific customer, technology, or situation. Capturing lessons learned on the project is a great way to provide this information to future teams. By gathering lessons learned and making them available to others, we can avoid learning things "the hard way."

There are several methods available to capture lessons learned, but we'll cover a couple that should be just enough for your projects.

Informal Approach. On most projects by the time the customer finally accepts the goods and services several members of the team have already been reassigned to other projects. To expect them to fill out a formal lessons-learned report is unrealistic. One easy, fun way to go about it is to combine the exercise with a project celebration. Get the team together for a pizza or drinks, and circulate among them, asking the one question shown just below. You'll be surprised at the valuable insights you'll get. Document the responses in a lessons-learned memo that you will send out to team members.

If you could pass one lesson you have learned from your experience on this project to a future team member, what would it be?

You will be amazed at the candid responses you get if you go about it this way. These are the real lessons, given when people have "let their hair down," that can be put to

DOCUMENT PREPARATION INFORMATION

PROJECT NAME	PREPARED BY (PRINT)	DATE PREPARED

PROJECT (CHECK OFF WHEN COMPLETE)

- ❑ Are any deliverables outstanding?
- ❑ Are there any internal outstanding commitments?
- ❑ Have all costs been appropriately charged to the project?
- ❑ Has the charge number from accounting been closed to prevent further charging against the project?
- ❑ Have all tasks been completed?
- ❑ Has management been notified regarding the availability of project personnel?
- ❑ Has management been notified regarding the availability of project facilities?
- ❑ Has excess project material been dealt with?
- ❑ Has the Project Plan been archived with all supporting information?
- ❑ Have suppliers been notified regarding any outstanding commitments?
- ❑ Are *all* stakeholders aware of project closeout?
- ❑ Has the project been transitioned to operations and support?
- ❑ (Add additional items unique to your project.)

PERSONNEL: INTERNAL

- ❑ Have you taken good care of high-performing project team members regarding future assignments?
- ❑ Have project team members been appropriately rewarded for their efforts if the project was successful?
- ❑ Was there a project celebration? Was it successful?
- ❑ (Add additional items unique to your project.)

EXTERNAL ISSUES

- ❑ Is a process in place for maintaining the customer relationship?
- ❑ Have vendors and subcontractors been advised of project status and of future opportunities?
- ❑ (Add additional items unique to your project.)

Figure 6-3. Project closeout checklist

immediate use in risk planning, team building, project planning and control, and customer relationship building. Of course, you do not want to attribute specific responses to specific people!

Formal Approach. On larger projects, the project manager will probably need to go a step beyond this informal method and compile a formal lessons-learned document. An example of an extensive, formal lessons-learned template is included in Figure 6-4. Even on smaller projects, this template provides a great list of "things to think about" when bringing the project to a close. Also, don't forgo the informal approach just because you use this checklist.

LESSONS LEARNED CHECKLIST

The purpose of the questionnaire is to help review the results from the project and to translate those results into lessons learned and recommendations for improvement.

GENERAL QUESTIONS	
Question	Response
Are you proud of our finished product or service?	
What was the single most frustrating part of our project?	
How would you do things differently next time to avoid this frustration?	
What was the most gratifying or professionally satisfying part of the project?	
Did the *Just Enough Project Management* process help? Which of the techniques worked particularly well for you?	
Which of the techniques were difficult or frustrating to use? What could be done to improve the process?	

Figure 6-4. Lessons-learned checklist (continued on next page)

STAKEHOLDER RELATIONSHIPS	
Question	**Response**
What difficulty did we have in working with other stakeholders?	
What difficulty did we have in working with other stakeholders?	
Did we have the right people assigned to all project roles? (Consider subject matter expertise, technical contributions, management, review and approval, and other key roles.) If not, how can we make sure that we get the right people next time?	
Did our stakeholders participate effectively? If not, how could we improve their participation?	
Were team members or necessary stakeholders missing from the kickoff meeting or other meetings? How can we avoid these oversights in the future?	
PROJECT INITIATION	
Did our requirements definition identify all the project deliverables we eventually delivered? Did the delivered product meet the specified project objectives? If not, what did we miss, and how can we be sure to capture necessary requirements on future projects?	
Did our requirements definition identify unnecessary deliverables? If so, how can we avoid this in the future?	
Did the Project Charter accurately capture all relevant information to successfully launch the project? If not, how can we do a better job in the future?	
PLANNING	
Were all team member and stakeholder roles and responsibilities clearly delineated and communicated? If not, how could we have improved these?	

Figure 6-4. Lessons-learned checklist (continued on next page)

PLANNING	
Question	**Response**
Were the project objectives broken down into tasks at the appropriate level? Was a complete work breakdown structure created? Was the schedule created using the WBS, and was all this information communicated to the appropriate team member or stakeholder? If not, how could we improve this?	
Was a project budget created using the WBS? If not, what formed the basis for estimating the project budget? What could we improve?	
Were risks identified and mitigated?	
Could we have completed this project without one or more of our vendors and/or contractors? If so, how?	
Were our constraints, limitations, and requirements made clear to all vendors and/or contractors from the beginning? If not, how could we have improved our statements of work?	
Was the internal resource assignment process adequate to identify and gain commitment for the right type and amount of resources for the project? If not, how could we improve?	
CONTROLLING	
Did we meet our schedule objectives? If not, why not, and how can we improve our schedule control process for future projects?	
Did we meet our cost objectives? If not, why not, and how can we improve our cost control process for future projects?	
Did we get timely, accurate feedback from the team and customer on the quality and timeliness of our deliverables? If not, how can we improve the process in the future?	

Figure 6-4. Lessons-learned checklist (continued on next page)

CONTROLLING	
Question	**Response**
Were our status reports produced on time, both from the team and to management? Were they helpful in monitoring the project? If not, why not?	
What worked well in the review and approval process?	
Was our process for managing change effective?	
CLOSING	
Did our hand-off to the customer represent a smooth and easy transition? If not, how could we have improved this process?	
Did we capture lessons learned from the teams?	
Did we recycle lessons learned in such a way that they can be accessed and used by future teams?	
Did we celebrate our success and reward team members appropriately? If not, why not? How can we ensure we give proper recognition in the future?	

Figure 6-4. Lessons-learned checklist (concluded)

Recycle Reusable Information. Once we've captured lessons learned, how do we ensure they are available to future teams? That, my friends, is the $64,000 question. There's no point in collecting lessons learned if they aren't used. Here are a couple of tricks I have learned to overcome this problem:

- **Establish an intranet site for lessons learned.** If you work in a large enough organization, this is a viable option. Set up the site, and tell everyone you know who has anything to do with projects about the site. Someone will have to post lessons learned to the site, but since it's in the project managers' best interests to learn from others' mistakes, they are motivated to post

the lessons. Of course, it works best if you have a project management office (PMO), but few organizations
have established PMOs. If you are lucky enough to
have a PMO, that organization maintains a file of lessons learned and also updates the project management
methodology (if you have one) to reflect best practices
gleaned from lessons learned.

- **E-mail everyone on the project team.** At a minimum,
  the project manager should e-mail the lessons learned
  to everyone on the project team and to others in the
  organization who are involved in projects.
- **Have the project manager and key team members
  attend future project planning sessions to pass on lessons learned in person.** This really works well! When a
  new team is brainstorming risks, it's the perfect time for
  the project manager to sit in and pass on the things that
  happened on a similar project. Some organizations have
  made this mandatory because it is so useful.

The least useful thing you can do is to write up a formal
lessons-learned report and file it in the project binder, with
no further action. Project managers don't have time to read
old project files. Sure, you should file a copy of the lessons
learned in the binder, but don't stop there—spread the word!

What happens when lessons learned are not gathered or
recycled for future use? We keep making the same dumb
mistakes over and over! Sorry to put it so bluntly, but it's
the truth. Here's an example. I once worked on a large project to develop a jam-proof communication system for use
by our troops during battle. The idea, of course, was to field
a system that protected our communications from eaves-
dropping by the "bad guys." This was, by the way, a couple
of decades ago.

Early in the program the Air Force and the Navy were
developing competing technologies. This was done on purpose so we could pick the more promising technology and
incorporate it into the system. Initial tests showed that one
of the technical approaches was superior and would be

ready before the other. The intelligent thing to do at that point would have been to make a decision to scrap the less promising technology and go with a single approach. But that didn't happen.

We proceeded into the prototyping phase. Both prototypes were developed and tested. We had experienced earlier that developing two parallel approaches was burning up our budget and stretching our resources thin, but we didn't learn that lesson. One of the prototypes (the one with the better technology) was superior, but, due to the politics involved, both programs were allowed to continue.

What happened as a result of not applying this obvious lesson? Ultimately both systems went into low-rate production and were fielded. The Navy used one, the other services the other. In an actual scenario in a far-off part of the world, the Navy and Air Force pilots were using different jam-proof systems so, in some cases, couldn't communicate! They were actually swapping information via floppy disk before the day's operations began. As a result of this fiasco, the Secretary of Defense killed one of the programs—but only after a lot of pain, wasted money, and operational difficulties. Today the problem has been fixed, but think of how much easier it would have been had we learned and applied our lesson earlier!

Celebrate. The final task for the project manager is to reward team members and have a little celebration to bring closure to the project and to the team. It's strange, but some project managers don't celebrate success—almost as if they are allergic to fun! Where is it written that project management has to be a drag? Go out and celebrate when you achieve something worthwhile! It's a good practice in life, too.

Bring Closure

We've discussed this as a basic human need. The project celebration, lessons-learned exercise, and a few words from the sponsor and project manager serve this purpose nicely.

The sponsor should let the team know how much their efforts are appreciated and the difference the project will make to the organization.

Communicate Achievements

There's an old country song with a lyric that goes something like this, "You can't be a beacon if your light don't shine." It doesn't matter how great the project team members performed if you don't tell the world about it. Remember the discussion about the esteem needs of most people on projects? Now is the time to let their light shine. Try these simple techniques:

- Publish the project results in the company newsletter, complete with pictures.
- Publish outstanding projects by submitting articles for publication in relevant trade journals and periodicals. For example, the Project Management Institute routinely publishes the results of outstanding project performance.
- Get the sponsor to give a short speech about the project at the next company "town meeting" or similar gathering.
- If you have internal broadcasts over a video system, ask the sponsor to acknowledge the team's effort using that forum.

Appreciate Everyone Involved

Finally, show the team that you appreciate their efforts. There are several effective ways to do this:

- **Throw a party!** We have talked about this throughout the book; now it's time to do it. People generally like to have fun, and we've already discussed how they value closure and want their efforts acknowledged. At a project celebration (please don't call it a "postmortem"—who would come to a party with a name like "postmortem"?) you, as the project manager, give a *short* speech acknowledging everyone's efforts, introduce the sponsor who does likewise, then relax, circulate, and conversationally capture a few lessons learned as we discussed earlier. Remember to have fun! Even if your organization doesn't allow project celebrations to be paid for out of company funds, the best project managers foot the bill themselves.

- **Write letters.** Take the time to write letters of appreciation to the team members' supervisors, with a copy to the individual. This simple technique accomplishes two purposes. First, it gives the individual a nice shot of esteem. Second, it gives their boss, who is probably a functional manager, something to put in the person's performance report. They will thank you for it. Be careful, however, not to write everyone a letter or to praise every person equally if he or she doesn't deserve it. Take care of the high performers, and work with the others to give honest feedback and suggestions for improving their performance. That is a gift, too.

Transition to Operations and Support and Maintenance

The project is finished! You have rewarded the team, closed the account, and made sure the customer is satisfied. One final check before you go to your next assignment is to make double sure that the deliverable and the customer are being supported by the operations division in your company.

How do you do this? If this is the first time this topic has come up, you're in trouble. The operations folks should have been identified as a key stakeholder when creating the Project Charter and given an opportunity to participate in project planning and control. They may not have attended every meeting, but when the subject of postproject support was on the agenda, they should have been there.

But assuming they have participated in the project to this point, your primary task is to make sure that the transition has occurred and there are no loose ends. Your main challenge may be to wean the customer away from the constant attention you have given them and prepare them for the kind of contact and support they will receive following project close. Thank goodness most of us work with account managers who take care of customer relationships before, during (to some extent), and after the project. Most organizations will handle many projects for long-term customers, so account managers are essential to keeping the customer from feeling neglected after the project team adjourns.

Once you have reassured yourself and the sponsor that the transition is complete, it's time to fold your tent and move on to the next project. Great job!

Managing Multiple Projects

Using *Just Enough Project Management* techniques you will be successful in managing single projects. But unfortunately most of us manage more than one project at the same time. How can we deal with this overload and successfully juggle many projects simultaneously? That is the topic of the final chapter—so read on for help in dealing with this challenging situation.

7

Juggling Multiple Projects and Dealing with Project Overload

ONE ARE THE DAYS WHEN WE STARTED AND FINISHED one project before beginning another one. That doesn't happen at home, at church, at school, or on the job. Like it or not, our reality involves juggling multiple projects simultaneously. What can we do, as a practical matter, to handle this situation? We must find a way to handle this overload, or we'll be at risk for burnout, despair, or being "downsized."

This chapter will equip you with the simple tools and techniques you can use to manage several projects at the same time and do it well—a little time management, some priority setting, and learning how to say no nicely. These well-known techniques will all contribute to a lower stress level and ultimately result in better project management across your organization.

Overload as the Norm

Overload has become the norm in most organizations. Communication overload, corporate overtime culture, and our inability or reluctance to say no get us into trouble. As we begin this discussion, it might be useful and revealing for you to think about how you currently handle overload.

Every organization I have dealt with since the turn of the century (the most recent one!) has increased the workload on its members. This is primarily due to the intense competitive pressure in the United States and abroad, coupled with pressure from shareholders and the market for ever-improving financial performance and growth.

In an effort to keep costs under control, management looks first at direct labor and its associated burden or indirect expense. Employee fringe benefits are costly. Each domestic employee must be provided benefits that include retirement plans, health care, dental care, vision care, life insurance, disability insurance, paid time off and vacations, and so on. Health care costs alone have risen dramatically on an annual basis for several years and show no sign of abatement. As a result, the pressure on management to reduce direct labor costs, with its associated indirect costs, has been intense. In companies with little growth, there have been dramatic layoffs. In companies with sustained growth, few or no jobs have been created to handle the additional work. The existing workforce has had to take on more. It's little wonder that many companies have outsourced some of their work overseas, where the expectations of the workforce are not as high.

As the president of a company myself, I have experienced this pressure firsthand. To maintain or increase market share, our company's products and services have to be at least as good as our competition's, and better in most cases. Most buying decisions these days are based on best value—the best technical solution at the best price. In a mature market, however, buyers don't differentiate among the competing products—they assume they are all good enough to meet their needs. That leads to intense pressure on price and cost management.

The upshot of all this is that management is reluctant to add people to the full-time staff. As business improves, the work is done by the same workforce, and, as a result, everyone has more work than he or she did in the "good old days." We need some practical tools to help us manage our increased workload. Adopting project management is, itself, one way we cope with doing more with less. Project teams are more efficient and effective than functional teams in handling project work. Assuming you employ the techniques described in this book to help you manage your individual projects, what else is available to help you juggle multiple projects and an overloaded schedule?

We can apply some simple techniques to help us first recognize, and then manage the overload. The Just Enough approach is not based on complicated software beyond that which most of us use every day anyway. With a stack of sticky notes and an honest appraisal of your workload, you will be able to apply this practical framework for managing your time—and your projects. These techniques work—it's up to you to put them into practice.

The Interconnectedness of It All

The first step toward juggling multiple projects is realizing that our projects are, in fact, interconnected. For years those of us in the project management education business strived to help people and organizations manage single projects more effectively. Now we are in an era where portfolio management is emphasized in many organizations.

A detailed treatment of portfolio—or program—management is beyond the scope of this book, but we can all apply some commonsense steps to help us manage our workload from the perspective that almost everything we do is related to something else we are working on. The various relationships among our projects and tasks may be described as *separate, dependent,* and *interdependent.*

Separate

In this scenario, we treat each project as a separate entity, as depicted in Figure 7-1. This perspective has the following characteristics:

Figure 7-1. Separate

- Each project is completely separate.
- There are no dependency relationships.
- There are no common resources.
- There are separate schedules.
- The projects are linked only because they have a common project manager.

This view is seldom accurate and could lead to trouble when we discover, for example, that our projects really do share resources. When a key person is delayed on one project and that delay impacts another project, we see that this view does not reflect the true relationship between the projects.

Dependent

In this scenario, projects are linked at the project level, as shown in Figure 7-2. In this view, projects A, B, C, and D are all separate projects but they are related in one of two ways:

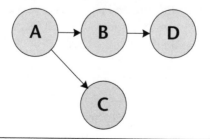

Figure 7-2. Dependent

- Projects may have a dependency relationship with another project. For example, maybe new technology being developed in project A is to be used in project B. If A is late, B will be late.
- Projects may have a common resource pool. If all four projects rely on the same talent pool, the risk is high that a key resource will not be available when needed.

Interdependent

Project tasks from one or more projects are linked as predecessors to tasks in other projects, as shown in Figure 7-3. If this is your reality, you are working in a very complex situation indeed. The following conditions prevail:

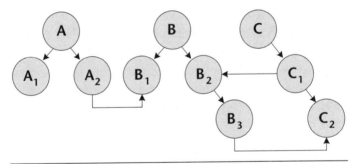

Figure 7-3. Interdependent

- Tasks among projects are linked. In Figure 7-3 you can see how A_2 and B_1 are linked. This could be a physical link, a resource dependency, a review point—lots of things. Maybe A_2 is a task to pour a concrete foundation for a basketball court, and task B_1 is to frame a small storage shed. Project A is the surface, project B is the building, and A_2 and B_1 are linked tasks. If A_2 is late, B_1 can't start on time, and so on.
- Projects may share the same resource pool, as described in the second scenario.

This situation is complex and difficult to manage, and it usually requires a more sophisticated approach, including software capable of tracking these linkages.

Conceptually, the best way to think about this last scenario is shown in Figure 7-4. Using this approach, the project manager is always aware of the interrelationships among projects and tasks. Team meetings take on a different tone as task managers and the project managers discuss progress at a variety of levels. The sense of awareness is heightened, and success is more likely.

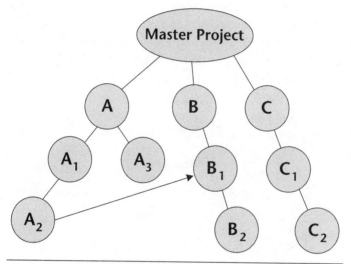

Figure 7-4. Master project

How can we treat all of our projects and tasks this same way without investing in expensive software or systems? It turns out the answer is easier than you might expect.

Five Steps to Coping with Project Overload

Help is on the way! The following five easy steps will help you manage overload and overlapping tasks. We'll cover each step in enough detail to enable you to put this model into practice immediately.

Step 1. List All Your Projects. The first step is to identify your current workload. If you haven't done so already, complete a project task worksheet for each project, but keep it at a high level at this point—at most the next five steps you will have to take to keep the project moving forward. If you have already completed detailed worksheets, that's great.

Next, transfer the name of each project to a sticky note and the phase or step that project is currently in (initiation, planning, control, or close). Stick the notes on a wall where they will not be removed until you remove them. Use a white board in your office or even a separate table—the important thing is to physically get them displayed in front of you. Include the information shown in Figure 7-5.

Project: _____

My Role: _____   Priority: _____

❑ Initiate
❑ Plan
❑ Control
❑ Close

Figure 7-5. Sticky note

There's not much point in recording more than your top five or six projects. We'll be operating under the *Pareto principle*—otherwise known as the *80–20 rule*. This states that 20 percent of your projects take up 80 percent of your time, cause 80 percent of your headaches, and so on. By concentrating on the top 20 percent of our projects and getting them under control, we will see an 80 percent improvement in overall results (and add a lot of peace and quiet to our lives!).

Step 2. Identify the Next Step for Each Project. If you have used the project task worksheet to create the WBS, you have before you all the tasks in each of the projects you just identified. Each task represents a step toward completing the project. If you haven't used the project task worksheet, fill one out now for your projects, as discussed above. Keep the level of detail relatively high, since we'll be looking at a fairly short time horizon in our planning efforts. At this point you might experience something interesting about how you view your workload.

In the decision sciences, it is a well-known phenomenon that simply giving structure to a problem is half its solution. In working with project overload, we can benefit from the same effect. Just looking at next steps can reduce an overload to a manageable size. Sometimes the work we haven't yet begun becomes, in our imagination, a huge undertaking. By bringing it out into the open, we see its real size and challenges.

A second point of identifying the next step in each of your top projects is to figure out exactly what needs to be done next. So jot down the next couple of steps for each of the projects you have identified on a sticky note, as shown in Figure 7-6. It's a good idea to put each of these "next steps" on a separate sticky notes so that you can move them around later.

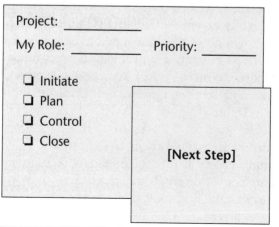

Figure 7-6. Next step

Step 3. Find the "Quick Hits." Using the following guidelines, identify which of the steps you have identified could result in the most immediate gain. Use the Pareto approach: Of the tasks you have identified, what are the 20 percent that would, if taken care of, give you an immediate substantial boost in gaining control of your overload?

1. Will a small investment of time keep the project moving?
2. Is the project near closure?
3. Are you stalled because you need a decision or lack clarity?

If the answer to any or all of these questions is yes, place these at the top of your list. Literally, take the sticky notes and begin to build a list of steps to take next. By doing it this way, you are crossing project boundaries and, in a very real sense, managing your entire project workload as a portfolio of interconnected tasks.

Step 4. Prioritize the Remaining Steps. The first thing to ask yourself is whether, after taking the quick hits out of the mix (we know we can get a lot of improvement by taking these immediately), are there any remaining steps we can eliminate or put on the back burner—ones that aren't as important as we first thought? Conversely, are there any that are really urgent and important that absolutely must get done right now? We'll use a grid to help us sort it out.

Figure 7-7 presents a matrix with urgency on one scale and importance on the other. Your next step is to take all the remaining steps and prioritize them using the matrix shown in Figure 7-7.

Tackle quadrant 1 tasks first—the most important, most urgent steps. Add them to the priority list you are developing. Next, identify the important steps in quadrant 2 that are not yet urgent. If we ignore these, they will soon become critical. Third, look at quadrant 3 steps that we can classify as urgent but that are not important. This is busy work we engage in because we don't have time for the

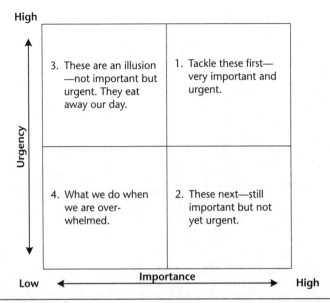

High

Urgency

3. These are an illusion —not important but urgent. They eat away our day.

1. Tackle these first— very important and urgent.

4. What we do when we are over- whelmed.

2. These next—still important but not yet urgent.

Low ← **Importance** → High

Figure 7-7. Matrix

important work—it seems too big to tackle given the small windows of time we have available. The beauty of these tasks is that you can usually safely put them on the back burner or ignore them since they are not important. Finally, look at quadrant 4 steps—not important and not urgent. When we are truly overwhelmed, we play solitaire on our pocket PCs or answer inane e-mails, or perhaps browse the World Wide Web. If you spend any of your time in quadrant 4, you really need this time management stuff!

When you're finished with this prioritization process, you should have all the steps displayed as shown in Figure 7-8.

Step 5. Schedule Your Time Weekly, and Be Able to Display Your Workload. Now that you have all the steps prioritized in a single list or arrangement of sticky notes, it is time to go to work. But wait! One more step before you leap into action. This will work for your current list of projects and next steps, but what about next week? And what happens

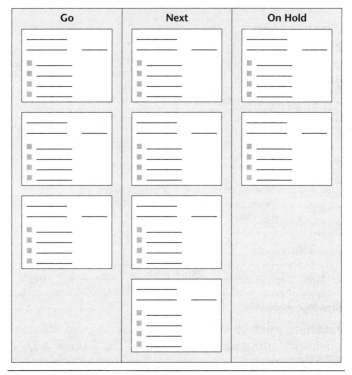

Figure 7-8. White board

when the boss drops another project onto your plate? Can this model help you? The answer is yes, but you must be able to demonstrate your workload so you can enter into a rational discussion.

The final step is to display your workload, either on a wall chart or on a computer using a tool like Microsoft *Outlook*. Personally, I use the *Outlook* task list feature for my projects and update it continuously when new tasks are added or drop off. I've seen others use a laminated wall chart and grease pencil. Still others prefer a *Word* document or *Excel* spreadsheet. It doesn't really matter as long as you can "prove" to someone who walks in the door with another hot project that you are already "maxed out." If you can point to your current list of tasks and specific steps you can then discuss what comes off the list if one more new project gets added—a completely different level of discussion than the usual emotional tirades we are sometimes forced into when we are overloaded and facing more work. Figure 7-9 shows a wall chart view of one person's workload.

Work Journal (or *Outlook* Calendar)

Scott Cook
Week of 11/16

Project	Planned Accomplishments	Actual
Brochure	1. Gather training opportunties	
Brochure	2. Write/collect descriptions	
Calendar	3. Finalize training calendar	
Goals	4. Meet with SR	

Daily Plan

Mon	Tues	Wed	Thur	Fri
Meeting on problems #1	#2 #3	Vendor meeting Staff meeting Planning	Dr.'s appt. Catch-up time!	#4 Review training calendar

---

Figure 7-9. Wall chart

Notice in Figure 7-9 that time has been added to the calendar for catch-up time on Thursday. It is just as important to build slack into your personal schedule as it is to include it in your project schedule. Otherwise you will not have time to recover from unexpected problems that will erode your plan.

One other thing: Make sure you add nonproject work to the calendar because, if you're like most of us, you have a mix of project and other work that fills your days. You might want to consider, as discussed above, a consolidated list of all projects and other work that takes up your time, as shown in Figure 7-10. This high-level view is most helpful in trade-off discussions as new work rolls into your already overcrowded schedule.

	Week 1	Week 2	Week 3
Project A	16 hr	10 hr	—
Project B	8 hr	4 hr	14 hr
Project C	—	20 hr	20 hr
Supervising	10 hr	10 hr	10 hr
Reports	3 hr	3 hr	3 hr
Miscellaneous	5 hr	5 hr	5 hr
TOTAL	42 hr	52 hr	52 hr

(Let the figures say no instead of you.)

Figure 7-10. Roll-up

The following list summarizes the five easy steps to managing project overload and juggling multiple projects:

1. List all your projects.
2. Identify the next step for each project.
3. Find the "quick hits."
4. Prioritize the remaining steps.
5. Schedule your time weekly and be able to display your workload.

As in the other techniques in *Just Enough Project Management*, these steps will work if you put them to use. The first time your boss walks in with a great new "opportunity" and you can engage in a rational discussion based on your demonstrated workload, you will feel that, just maybe, you are getting a handle on your overloaded work life.

One more quick story before we're done. Recently my boss called me with a good news/bad news scenario. The bad news was that one of the division presidents had unexpectedly resigned, and in the aftermath, it was discovered that many of the projects in this organization were "challenged" in some way—some were behind schedule, some were over budget, and some were not achieving their technical objectives. I was asked to lend a hand and apply some of the material in this book to these projects, conduct some training, and help the division get control of their projects. More bad news was that I was already overloaded and had no time in my schedule.

The good news was this: As I always do, I was using the techniques in this book on a daily basis. So instead of "flying off the handle" with exclamations that I couldn't possibly take on any more work, I opened my task list (which I maintain religiously on *Outlook*), and my boss and I entered into a constructive dialog on which of the projects listed could be shifted to others, which could be allowed to slip, and which were no longer even a high priority. Nice discussion, no hard feelings, and the work needed in a sister division got done.

So once again and in closing, I encourage you to put these simple steps into action. You will experience better results and get control of your projects!

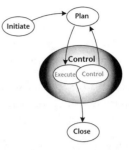

Glossary

THIS GLOSSARY CONTAINS A WIDE VARIETY OF PROJECT management terms, many of which do not appear in the *Just Enough Project Management* lexicon. Many readers will be involved in more complex projects where some of the project management jargon in use on larger projects may be used; therefore, more definitions, rather than fewer, are included here.

activity An element of work performed during the course of a project. An activity normally has an expected duration, expected cost, and expected resource requirements. In *Just Enough Project Management*, the terms *activity* and *task* are used interchangeably.

activity description A name that easily identifies an activity with an element of the WBS.

actual finish date The calendar date on which work actually ended on an activity. It must be equal to or after the start date.

actual start date The calendar date on which work actually began on an activity. It must be prior to or equal to the finish date.

assumption A statement that is perceived to be correct at the time it is made.

baseline A management-approved Project Plan fixed at a specific point in time in the project life cycle and used to measure the progress of the project. A set of data used for comparison or control.

bottom-up estimating The process of developing an estimate in which the total estimate is the sum of estimates of all tasks in the WBS.

budget An estimate of funds planned to cover a project or specified period of future time.

budgeting Part of the planning function and control mechanism for a project.

change An alteration in any of the project characteristics.

change management process A set of tasks or procedures established to ensure that changes are reviewed, approved, or rejected and the baseline updated.

change request A formal written statement asking to make a modification to some element of the Project Plan or specifications.

conflict management The process the project manager uses to deal with the inevitable differences that occur on a project team.

conflict resolution The process of seeking a solution to a problem.

constraints Factors that will limit the project management team's options—for example, a predefined budget, deadlines, technology choices, or legislative action.

contingency planning The process of identifying and planning appropriate responses to be taken when, and if, a risk actually occurs.

contract A binding agreement between two or more parties that establishes the requirements for the products and services to be acquired.

corrective action Action necessary to correct variance from the Project Plan.

crashing An action to decrease the duration of an activity on the critical path by increasing the expenditure of resources.

critical path A sequential path of activities in a network schedule that represents the longest duration of a project. Any slippage of the tasks in the critical path increases the duration of the project unless corrective action is taken.

critical success factors Factors necessary to ensure the success of the project's design, development, and implementation. They are based on the customer's view of the project.

current estimate A forecast of start and finish dates, hours of effort, and cost, that is made at any time after the baseline start date has passed.

deliverable A tangible product or service that satisfies one or more project objectives.

detailed schedule A schedule used to communicate the day-to-day tasks to project team members working on the project.

duration The amount of time a task or the project will take, either planned or actual. Duration can be stated with or without inclusion of nonwork time.

estimate An evaluation of all the cost elements of a project or effort as defined by an agreed-upon scope.

estimate at completion The value (expressed in dollars and/or hours) developed to represent a realistic appraisal of the cost of the project once it is completed. It takes into consideration actual cost, plus projected cost, and it is an assessment of the total project effort.

feasibility studies The methods and techniques used to examine technical and cost data to determine the economic potential and the practicality of a project.

feedback Information extracted from a process or situation and used in controlling, planning, or modifying immediate or future inputs to the project.

float See *slack*.

functional manager A manager responsible for activities in a specialized department or area.

functional organization Any group outside of the project manager's control that is responsible for tasks in the work breakdown structure.

Gantt chart Graphic representation of a project schedule that shows each job as a bar whose length is proportional to its duration. The bars appear in rows and indicate the task start and end times as well as overlaps with other tasks.

impact The loss or effect on the project if the risk occurs.

initiation See *project initiation*.

lessons learned Documented information usually collected through meetings, discussions, or written reports to capture team members' perceptions of successes and mistakes in the project as well as processes that worked well or need attention.

management reserve An amount of time or funds set aside for contingencies.

matrix organization A project organization form in which resources are "loaned" to the project on a temporary basis. The project manager and the functional manager share authority over the resources. The balance of power in a matrix depends on whether it is a strong or weak matrix. In a *strong matrix* the project manager exercises more control while in a *weak matrix* the functional manager has the power.

milestone A task with zero duration and requiring no resources, used to measure the progress of a project and signify completion or start of effort to produce a deliverable.

network diagram A schematic display of the sequential and logical relationship of the tasks in the WBS.

PMBOK® Guide The *Project Management Body of Knowledge* is an inclusive term that describes the sum of knowledge within the profession of project management as defined by the Project Management Institute (PMI).

probability The chances that a risk event will occur.

process The set of activities performed for a given purpose.

product General term used to define the end result of a project delivered to a customer.

program A group of interrelated projects managed as an entity in a coordinated way. While programs have finite start dates, they may last for years or indefinitely.

program evaluation and review technique (PERT) A task-oriented project scheduling technique used to estimate overall project duration when there is uncertainty in the individual activity duration estimates. PERT uses durations that are computed by calculating the weighted average of optimistic, pessimistic, and most-likely duration estimates for each task to estimate the project duration. Using PERT, the project end date can be stated in probabilistic terms, and the confidence intervals can be defined based on the standard deviations of the tasks on the critical path.

progress report A report comparing actual progress with the current, approved baseline plan.

project Any undertaking with *defined starting and ending points* and *specific, well-defined objectives* that, when attained, identify completion.

project binder Also known as the *project repository*. The physical location of all project-specific documentation, including the Project Charter, Project Plan, status reports, and contract if applicable. May be wholly or partially electronic.

project budget The amount and distribution of money allocated to a project over time.

project change An approved change to an element of the project work.

Project Charter The deliverable from the project initiation process. A document that concisely describes the project, announces the appointment of the project manager, provides organizational authority to apply resources to the project, and provides authority to proceed with project planning.

project closing A process that provides for acceptance of the project by the project sponsor, recycling of lessons learned on the project, and reward and recognition for project achievements.

project duration The elapsed time from the project start date to the project finish date.

project initiation The process of formally launching a project. This process consists of verifying that all stakeholders have been identified, that all the information needed to begin the project is documented in the Project Charter, that the project manager has been appointed and vested with the requisite authority to carry out the project, and that the charter was approved by the project sponsor.

project life cycle A collection of phases through which any project passes. Note that the number of phases and the breakdown are dependent on the methodology being used. The Just Enough Project Management life cycle consists of project initiation, project planning, project control, and project close.

project management Informally defined as "getting the job done on time, within budget, according to the specifications." A more formal definition is "the application of knowledge, skills, tools, and techniques to project activities in order to meet or exceed the stakeholder's needs and expectations from a project."

project manager The individual appointed and given responsibility for the overall success of the project.

project objectives A description of the specific outcomes that the project intends to accomplish. Project objectives should be specific, measurable, agreed, realistic, and time constrained (SMART).

Project Plan A formal, approved document used to manage and control project tasks and activities.

project planning The identification of the project objectives, tasks, schedule, resources, costs, risks, communications, and other elements necessary to complete a project.

project schedule A graphical representation of predicted tasks, milestones, dependencies, resource requirements, task durations, and deadlines.

project sponsor Individual manager for whom the project is being undertaken. This person will be responsible for the commitment of the resources required to conduct the project, budgeting the funds to undertake the project, and exercising final decision authority on the project.

resource planning Determining what resources (people, equipment, materials) are needed in what quantities to perform project tasks.

risk An event or condition that, should it occur, could have an adverse effect on project objectives. (Note, the *PMBOK Guide* states that the impact could be positive or negative.)

risk event An occurrence that may negatively affect a project.

risk management The art and science of identifying, analyzing, and responding to risk factors throughout the life of a project.

scheduling The recognition of realistic time and resource restraints that will, in some way, influence the execution of the plan.

scope The work content and products of a project or component of a project. The scope names all activities performed, the resources consumed, and the end products that result, including quality standards.

slack Also known as *float*. The amount of time a task may be delayed from its early start without delaying the project finish date.

sponsor See *project sponsor*.

stakeholders Individuals or organizational entities who are involved in or may be affected by project activities.

status reports Reports produced at predefined intervals to provide information on the project.

strategy A framework for guiding choices that determine the nature and direction needed to attain an objective.

task See *activity*.

team building The process of influencing a group of diverse individuals, each with individual goals, needs, and perspectives, to work together effectively to achieve a stated objective.

team member Any individual, reporting either part time or full time to the project manager, who is responsible for some aspect of the project's activities.

time management The knowledge required to ensure timely completion of the project—consisting of task definition, sequencing, duration estimating, schedule development, and schedule control.

variance The difference between planned and actual results, expressed in the formula $V = P - A$. A variance can positive or negative.

work breakdown structure (WBS) A task-oriented hierarchical depiction of activities that organizes, defines, and displays the total work to be accomplished to achieve the objectives of a project. Each descending level represents an increasingly detailed definition of the project objective. The WBS includes all project work, and it is a tool for subdividing a project into manageable work elements that can be assigned to individuals or to organizational entities who will be held accountable for performance of assigned elements as detailed in the Project Plan.

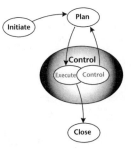

Further Reading

MOST BIBLIOGRAPHIES ARE BORING LISTS OF BOOKS THAT most people won't read. The books listed in this bibliography are different in that they have either endured for years and still provide sound advice on how to get better project results or they are new and insightful—and they are also helpful in improving project performance. So if you want to improve your project results and the body of *Just Enough Project Management* hasn't given you everything you need, try one of the books listed here. If you still have questions, e-mail me at **curtcook@skybest.com**, and I can probably hook you up with the author so you can discuss your problem.

Augustine, Norman R., and Harvard Business Review, *Managing Projects and Programs* (Boston: Harvard Business School Press, 1989). This is an "oldie but goodie," and, let's face it, to get into the *Harvard Business Review* in the first place, an author has to have something to say. If you are a professional project manager, this should be on your shelf. If not, it's still interesting reading on the underlying concepts of project management.

Baker, Sunny, and Kim Baker, *The Complete Idiot's Guide to Project Management* (New York: Alpha Books, 1998). This is the funniest book on project management I've ever read (but of course, there's not much competition in that category!). One of my favorite lines, which I use often, is from page 30: "Agreeing to do the impossible still leaves whatever you agreed to, well, impossible!"

Cleland, David I., and Lewis R. Ireland, *Project Management: Strategic Design and Implementation*, 4th ed. (New York: McGraw-Hill, 2002). First published by TAB Books and authored by David Cleland in 1990, this book ties projects to corporate and business unit strategic objectives. Without this linkage, why do the project?

Cleland, David I., and William R. King, *Systems Analysis and Project Management*, 3rd ed. (New York: McGraw-Hill, 1983). Cleland and King wrote the original book in 1968, and it received the McKinsey Foundation Award. The beauty of this book is its systems orientation to project management. It recognizes that projects are always part of something larger and that we will be more successful if we recognize that fact and look for the interrelationships right off the bat, during project planning. Today we call that program "portfolio management" and wonder how to do it—but here's a book written 26 years ago that tells us how!

Cleland, David I., and William R. King, *Project Management Handbook*, 2nd ed. (New York: Van Nostrand Reinhold, 1988). The first edition, published in 1983, was selected as the Institute of Industrial Engineers' Book-of-the-Year award. This is probably the seminal reference guide for project managers, and it continues to provide many of us with useful information on the entire spectrum of project management. Part of its value lies in the fact that many of the great minds in the evolution of project management contributed to the work—people like Russell Archibald, Linn Stuckenbruck, William King, John Adams, and of course David Cleland.

Collins, James C., *Good to Great* (New York: HarperCollins, 2001). Almost everything in *Good to Great* can be applied to projects just as easily as to organizations. Read what he says about "first who, then what" and you will understand the importance of getting the best people on your project team. Then take his advice on how to lead these mustangs and you will achieve project success!

Covey, Stephen R., *The Seven Habits of Highly Effective People* (New York: Simon & Schuster, 1989). There's not much to add to the accolades this book has received. It's listed here because it's a classic on how to achieve success—whether you're a project manager or the captain of a ship. Also, in Chapter 7 on juggling multiple projects, I used a grid to prioritize project steps, and this came in large part from Covey's work.

Frame, J. Davidson, *Managing Projects in Organizations* (San Francisco: Jossey-Bass, 2002). David Frame will tell you he wrote this book in hotel rooms while traveling around the world delivering a seminar of the same name. He was one of my early mentors while pursuing my doctorate at George Washington University, and I taught his seminar dozens of times using this book. Obviously I liked it! It's a quick read, full of useful and amusing anecdotes on how to avoid the pitfalls in managing projects large and small.

Harvard Business Review, *Project Management: A Harvard Business Review Paperback* (Boston: Harvard Business School Press, 1991). Even though this collection is 13 years old, the articles from some of the early thinkers in the field provide excellent coverage of a wide range of project topics, from strategy and risk to how to create and manage a project team and when to kill a project. Everything in this volume is still relevant and useful today. I especially like Paul O. Gaddis' article entitled "The Project Manager." Unfortunately, this is out of print, but you might be able to get a copy via the Internet.

Jain, Raj K., and Harry C. Triandis, *Management of Research and Development Organizations: Managing the Unmanageable*, 2nd ed. (New York: Wiley & Sons, 1997). In a world where being first to market with a breakthrough product could mean the difference between survival and bankruptcy, R&D organizations cannot afford to turn researchers loose to pursue their individual lines of research. Commercialization is the name of the game, and management of R&D efforts as projects applies just the right amount of accountability and rigor to dramatically improve the success rate. This book by Jain and Triandis is simply the best treatment of the topic I have seen. If you are in research and development, you owe it to yourself to read it.

Katzenbach, Jon R., and Douglas K. Smith, *The Discipline of Teams* (New York: Wiley & Sons, 2001). This book is all about maximizing the performance of small groups. For example, an early statement gives the reader an insight into the importance of stating the project objective as a performance challenge: "A common performance objective is much more motivating for effective teams than the desire to be a team." It's not about rahrah, sis boom bah—it's about achieving something challenging and worthwhile. That is what helps form a group of individuals into a team. If you are having trouble creating and motivating project teams, this book will provide practical measures that will make a difference.

Kerzner, Harold, *Project Management: A Systems Approach to Planning, Scheduling, and Controlling*, 7th ed. (New York: Wiley & Sons, 2001). OK, I haven't read the whole 1,203 pages, but then, who has? Kerzner's book has checklists for everything—and they are very useful when you need a specific solution to a problem. This is an excellent reference text. I like the in-depth coverage of the project sponsor's roles and responsibilities.

Leech, D. J., and B. T. Turner, *Project Management for Profit* (Chichester, England: Ellis Horwood, 1990). I have been using this book for my seminars and writing since it came out in 1990. Its focus is on large, contracted projects from a very pragmatic perspective—how to make money on them! It's refreshing, practical, and engaging. Unfortunately it is out of print, but you might be able to get a copy via the Internet.

Lewis, James P., *Project Leadership* (New York: McGraw-Hill, 2003). Dr. Jim Lewis holds a Ph.D. in psychology, so he knows what he's talking about when it comes to human behavior. In *Project Leadership* he does an excellent job of explaining the connection between project leadership and personality types, leadership styles, and communication—but what I really like about this book is his discussion of Daniel Goleman's research and theories on the importance of developing people's emotional intelligence in the workplace (and on projects). (Goleman, *Working with Emotional Intelligence*, Bantam Books, 1998.)

Lewis, James P., *Project Planning, Scheduling & Control*, 3rd ed. (New York: McGraw-Hill, 2001). At 550 pages, Jim Lewis' book goes *way* beyond the detail I've provided on scheduling and controlling projects. The nice thing about Jim's books is the upbeat and humorous way he explains serious topics.

Project Management Institute (PMI) Standards Committee, *A Guide to the Project Management Body of Knowledge* (Upper Darby, PA: Project Management Institute, 2001). The *PMBOK*, as it is commonly known, is the American National Standards Institute standard for managing projects in the United States. While it's not the most scintillating reading, no project manager should be without a copy.

Tobin, James, *Great Projects* (New York: Free Press, 2001). This is the most interesting book on project management I have ever read … probably because it's not about projects but about America and building things—great things that have been central to our nation's experience and growth. You will find behind-the-scenes stories ranging from the harnessing of the Mississippi to the building of the country's great dams and Boston's Big Dig to the creation of the Internet. Fascinating stuff—you'll enjoy it.

Ward, J. LeRoy, *Project Management Terms: A Working Glossary* (Arlington, Va.: ESI International, 2000). LeRoy Ward has put together the best working glossary of all the weird and peculiar terms project managers use ("How's your budgeted cost of work scheduled today, and oh, how about that to-complete-performance-index?"). This is a good reference book and more extensive than the official version published by the Project Management Institute.

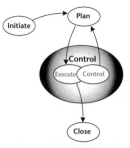

Index

About the Author

Curtis R. Cook, Ph.D., PMP, is president of Novations Project Management in Atlanta. He is responsible for achieving business results through the development and implementation of projects, people, and processes. His background includes P&L responsibility in a number of training and consulting firms, as well federal government organizations. He is known for his technical expertise and experience in consulting, mentoring, coaching, training, strategic planning, and organizational development. Dr. Cook has presented seminars in 35 countries to thousands of executives, managers, and team members in virtually all industry sectors, including information technology, architect/engineering, pharmaceuticals, biotechnology, construction, government, aerospace/defense, oil/energy, product development, and general services. In total, Dr. Cook has more than 30 years' experience in managing private and public-sector organizations, projects, and contracts. He holds a Ph.D. from George Washington University, an MBA from the University of Utah, and a bachelor's degree from the University of Oklahoma. He is a Certified Project Management Professional (PMP) and a Certified Professional Contracts Manager (CPCM).